AF378499

THE STORY OF NFTs

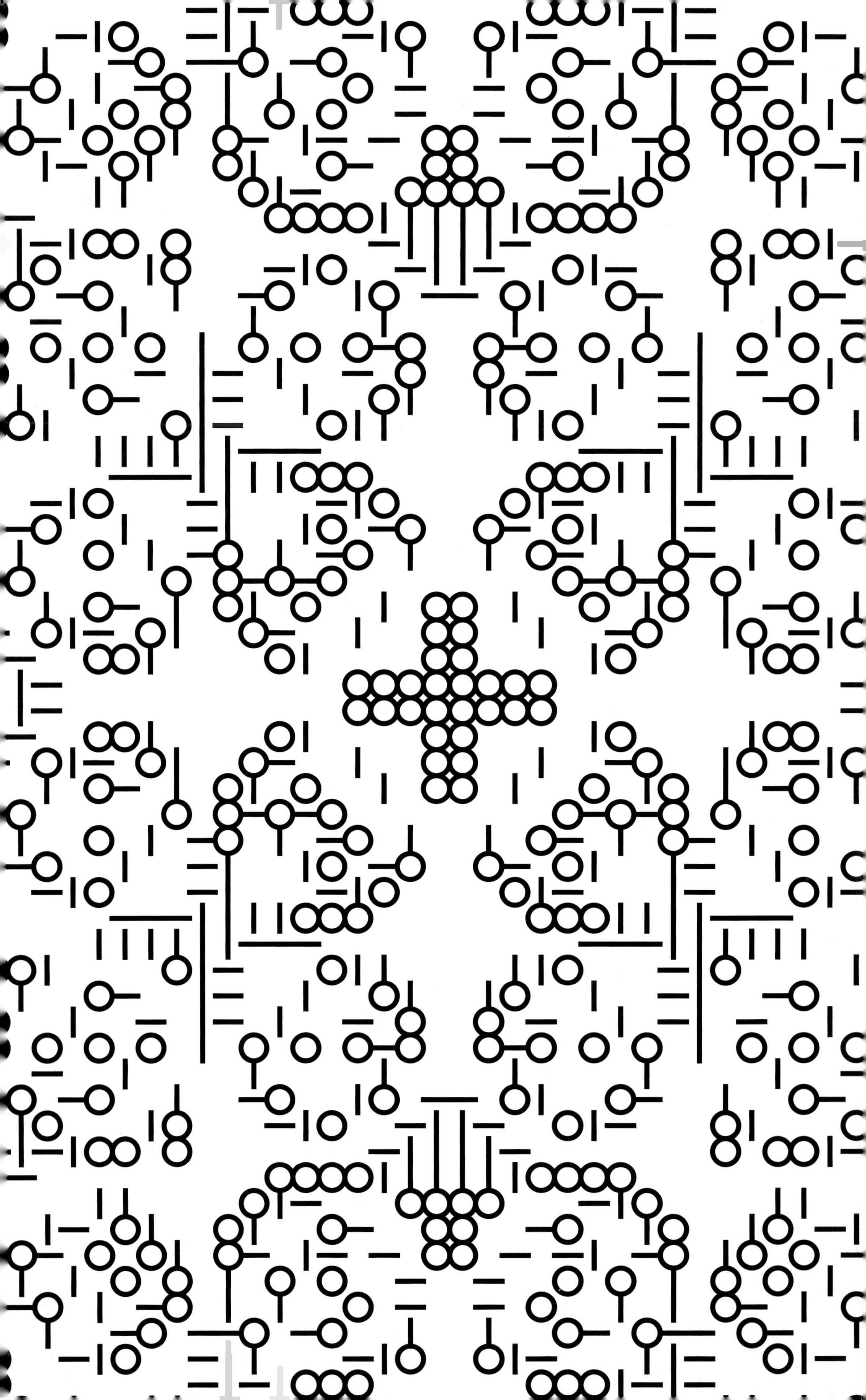

THE STORY OF NFTs

Artists, Technology, and Democracy

Amy Whitaker &
Nora Burnett Abrams

Rizzoli **Electa**

MCA
DENVER

CONTENTS

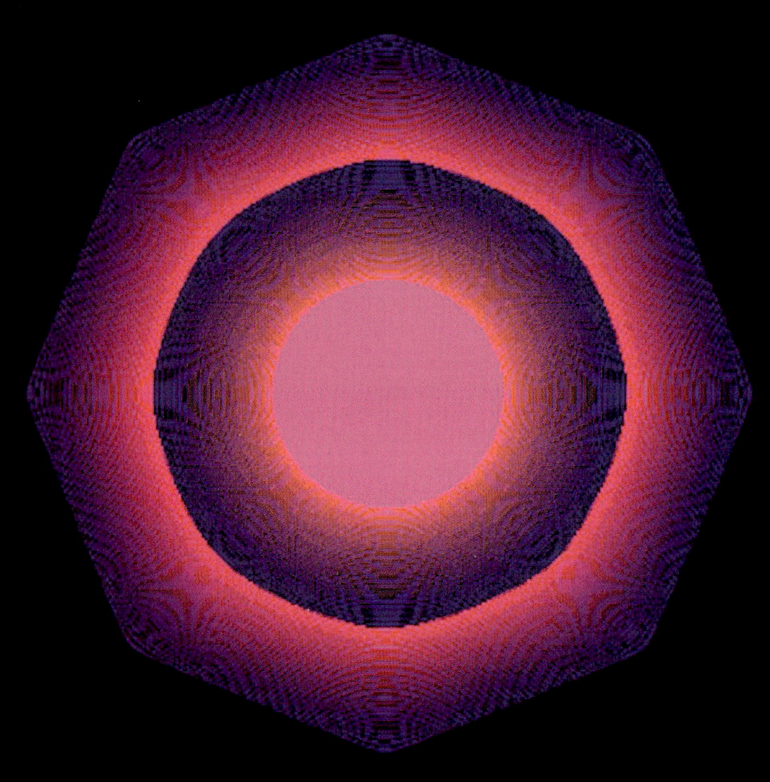

INTRODUCTION

We are just completing a thirty-year arc of digitization. Now we are beginning a thirty-year arc of tokenization.

KEVIN McCOY, ARTIST

IN THE EARLY DAYS OF THE COVID pandemic, artists were making new digital works registered to the decentralized ledger of blockchain, while many museums were selling physical artworks—paintings, drawings, sculptures. The Association of Art Museum Directors (AAMD), the governing body of art museums in the United States, had issued a landmark decision to loosen temporarily its deaccessioning policy for two years, enabling a museum to sell artworks from its holdings and to use those funds "to support the direct care of the museum's collection," rather than solely for the acquisition of other works of art, as had been the policy for decades. This shift in policy, which effectively allowed museums to sell from their collections to cover operating expenses, encapsulates two different threads of this book: the complex dynamic between art and finance, and the larger relationship of capitalism and democracy. Especially in the seeming post-truth age of social media, money in politics, and eroded trust in institutions, the story of NFTs—non-fungible tokens—and blockchain across museums, art markets, and creative practice has something to tell us not only about the arts but also about the future we want to live in.

The ramification of AAMD's policy shift was to enable museums facing devastating financial strain to stabilize parts of their operations, but it also raised existential questions about the long-term

Fig. 1
Kevin McCoy,
Quantum,
2014–21. Jpeg
and associated
non-fungible
token (token
ID: 0).

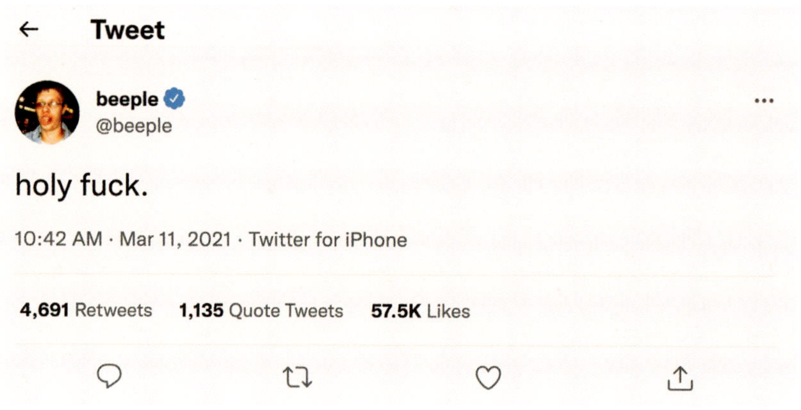

← **Tweet**

beeple ✓
@beeple

···

holy fuck.

10:42 AM · Mar 11, 2021 · Twitter for iPhone

4,691 Retweets   **1,135** Quote Tweets   **57.5K** Likes

Fig. 2
A tweet by Beeple (Mike Winkelmann) after the sale of his NFT for 69.346 million dollars, 2021.

complexity of museums' seemingly singular focus on collection building and collection maintenance. Responses to these questions reflected a range of perspectives—from a more traditional view of museums as guardians of history to a more progressive, restructured, and even speculative view of shared ownership of history and, relatedly, novel approaches to supporting artists' work without the burden museums face of storing and conserving artworks in perpetuity.

Concurrent with—or brought to the fore by—these financial strains, museums were also confronted with an even larger existential question about their relevance other than as repositories of objects: Museums, historically colonialist and often exclusionary institutions, could no longer avoid the call to live in the world as equitable, diverse, and inclusive organizations. Centuries of ambivalence and avoidance of honestly and authentically creating spaces of inclusion and accessibility telescoped to an urgent reckoning with racial injustice, and cultural institutions were called upon to respond in structural, not merely symbolic, ways to their own histories and current contexts. In the wake of George Floyd's murder on May 25, 2020, such struggles surfaced with renewed urgency across the museum field.

Discussions of deaccessioning quickly became enmeshed in the context of diversity and equity. In some instances, the motivation for deaccessioning became inseparable from calls for greater resources to be directed to communities of color, to artists of color, and to museums' own BIPOC (Black, Indigenous, and People of Color) staff. Museums—notably the Baltimore Museum of Art—developed plans to sell works in their collections by predominantly White, Western men in order to raise funds for initiatives and programs that would now center people of color. A pivotal convening in March 2021, organized by Syracuse University, brought these many perspectives to bear on one another, while also raising questions around the value proposition that was being put forward: In the words of the artist Carrie Mae Weems, why did acquiring the work of women artists and artists of color have to

1983
Apple IIe computer
released

come at the expense of other works of art? Why was the expansion of museum collections a question of either/or rather than both/and?[1]

About a week before this symposium launched, a different event punctured the ecosystem of the contemporary art world: Beeple—the artist also known as Mike Winkelmann—sold his NFT *Everydays: The First 5000 Days* at Christie's auction house for 69.346 million dollars (Fig. 3). The fact of any work selling for that much money caught the attention of many outside of the art world, but the success of this sale seemed to catch those practicing within the traditional art world off-guard. The sale brought both a record price—the third-highest auction result for a living artist—and a collision of seemingly unrelated fields that destabilized the pillars of the contemporary art world. As an artist operating outside the mainstream of the art market and related museum and gallery ecosystem, Beeple had amassed a notable Instagram following.

Other artists working on Instagram had amassed social-media followings and art sales as well, but without anything like the scale of Beeple's auction sale. Notably, Elise Swopes, one of the very first artists to join Instagram after the platform launched in 2010, sold her first NFT (Fig. 4) in the same month as the Beeple sale—for 17,600 dollars—and went on to sell 200,000 dollars in NFTs that year, a significant sum but orders of magnitude from the Beeple result. It is the auction and price tag itself—not the art—that brought Beeple's work to broad relevance and landed an image of the work across the cover of the *Wall Street Journal*. Profuse coverage of the sale catapulted the conversation well beyond the art world. The artist's own response over Twitter summed up the same more succinctly than anyone else could have (Fig. 2).

The purchaser of the Beeple was Vignesh Sundaresan, who goes by MetaKovan, and he was buying the work on behalf of a fund called Metapurse in order to divide the work immediately into salable, fractional shares. Beeple's NFT entered the cultural zeitgeist, and blockchain-registered artworks—which had been circulating for several years but were now broadly labeled NFTs—launched a tug-of-war between a more niche cultural community and the traditional taste-making apparatus and vetting systems of both the art market and the museum ecosystem. Beeple's work itself was objectionable; critic Ben Davis analyzed the individual daily works that made up the 5,000 "everydays" in detail and found many of them to be, at turns, racist, sexist, or homophobic. Davis, who called the result a "stomach-turning auction price" in *Artnet News,* wrote that at his most successful, Beeple is a "digital satirist" commenting on "incipient tech dystopia and political outrages," but that he was also "mainly reflect[ing] the shrieking, Trump-era vitriol of cable news or Facebook comment wars, without any particular stable point of view."[2]

The importance of the work is its impact on the market and the way its meteoric price has ushered in a presumption regarding the significance of NFTs. The sale

1989
15% of U.S. households
have a computer

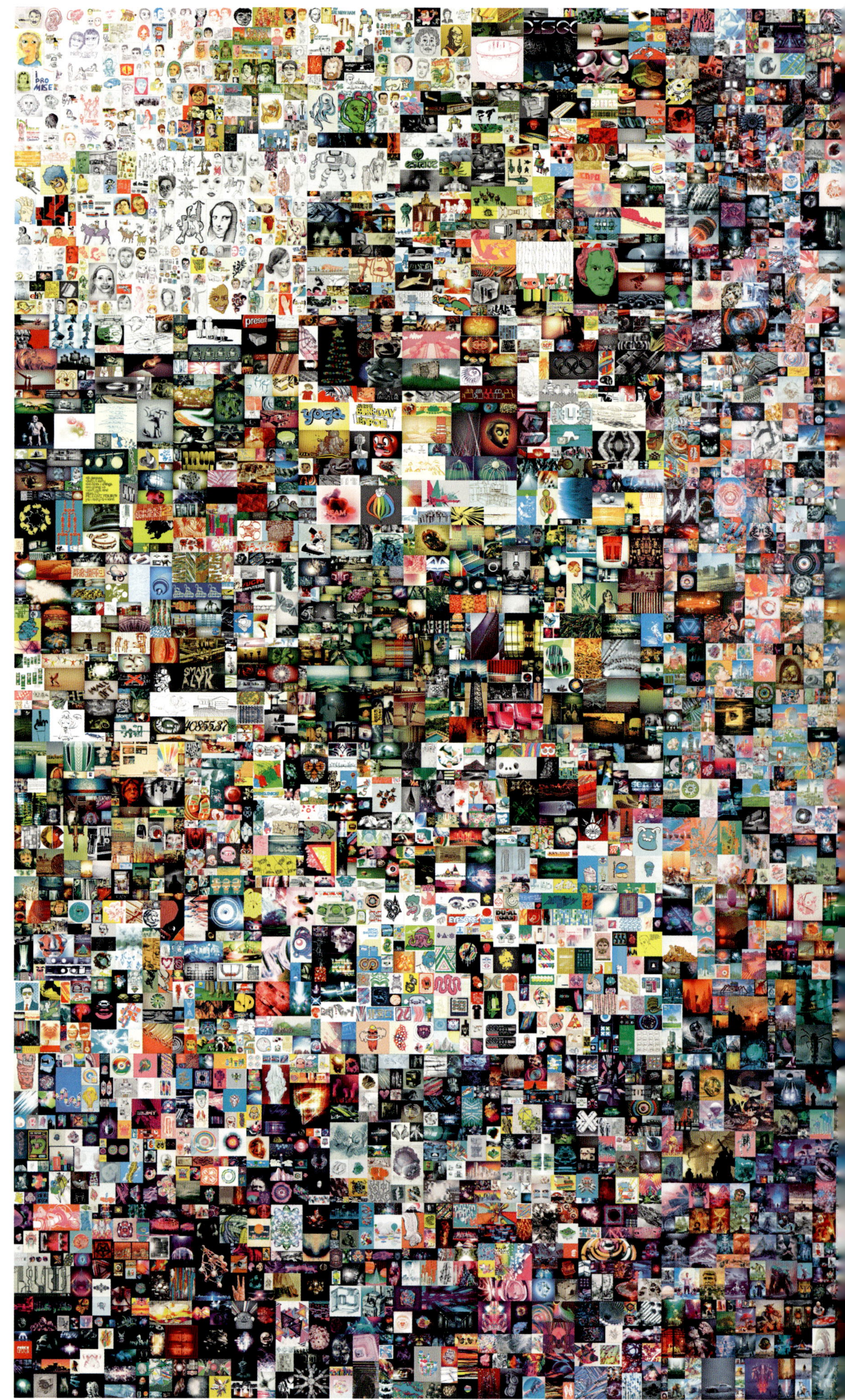

11

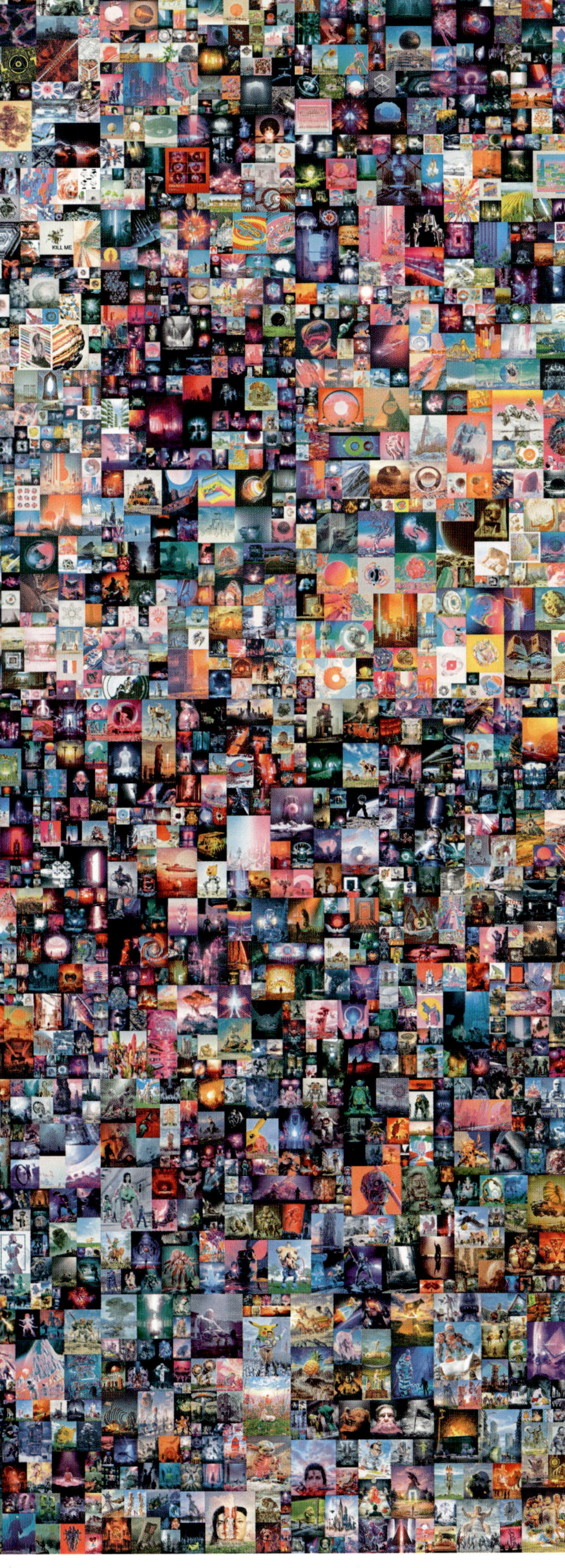

Fig. 3
Beeple (Mike Winkelmann), *Everydays: The First 5000 Days*, 2021. Jpeg and associated non-fungible token (token ID: 40913).

also posed unavoidable and important questions about the future of contemporary art—particularly related to artistic practice and collecting—and the relevance of museums as institutions dedicated to advancing and celebrating creativity. Our interest resides in these questions about the future, and a sense of urgency—but infinitely more so, a sense of importance—about the invitation to participate in how blockchain and NFTs could reshape the arts and the larger world, including revitalizing the democratic projects of both.

The intersection of these questions is where our collaboration came together. In March 2021, a close mutual friend, the museum director Veronica Roberts, put us into conversation—one with questions to raise and the other with the expertise to address these questions holistically and specifically. Whitaker had been researching blockchain since 2014—both commercially and through artists' activism around property—and Abrams brought a museum leader's eye to cutting a clean line through a messy field full of performative expertise, pat-on-the-head assurances that something was too complicated, and avoidance from some traditional museum corners.

We began by trying to understand NFTs not as an alien landing but instead as part of the history of art—for instance, a continuation of Sol LeWitt's conceptual art practice dating to the late 1960s and early 1970s and his use of certificates of authenticity to guarantee that a work by him was in fact a work of his. At the same time, especially in the context of conversations around diversity, equity, and inclusion, it was generative to consider some of the radically expansive possibilities of blockchain technology. These questions at the heart of artistic practice—how artists circumventing commercial markets have historically been and continue to be subsumed by them, or how artists have retained authority over their work—invite profound ways of reimagining artists' livelihoods, institutions' collections, and, beyond that, the democratic possibilities of blockchain technology itself. From here, a collaboration was born.

We first hosted a spring 2021 online public program at the Museum of Contemporary Art Denver, aptly titled "NFTs-WTF?" We tried to place NFTs in the history of art: Were they part of conceptual, even market-avoidant artistic practice? Or, with escalating prices and marquee sales overtaking financial news coverage, were they a reprise of the go-go 1980s art market in its ascendency? Perhaps both?

The conversational space between us—a museum director and curator and a longtime blockchain researcher and professor—fueled a larger journey of curiosity across many different parts of the NFT story. What seemed initially to be about money and technology was also clearly about art and democracy. The contours of the NFT phenomenon were hard to map because they were changing so rapidly, but what we could see was a set of intersecting stories—art stories, artist

Fig. 4
Elise Swopes, *Where Focus Goes, Energy Flows*, 2021. Video (mp4) created on an iPhone.

1991
Stuart Haber and Scott Stornetta publish "How to Time-Stamp a Digital Document" in the *Journal of Cryptology*

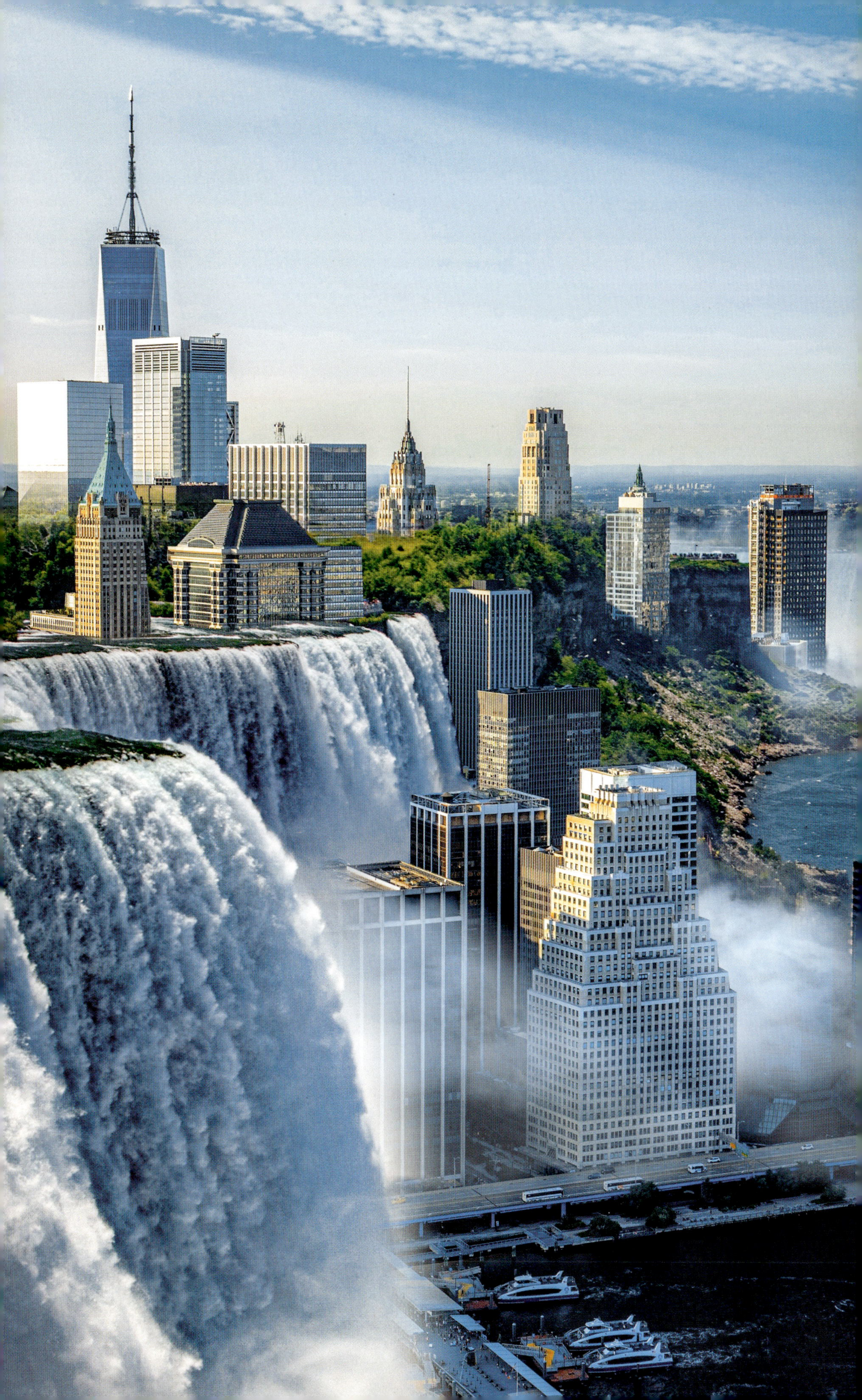

stories, democracy stories, technology stories, knowledge stories, and money stories. And these stories offered a lens through which to see the origins, the value, and the potential of blockchain and the non-fungible tokens registered to it.

We found that the people most deeply engaged in the technology were so constantly learning that they were unafraid to say they didn't know. We also found many brilliant people who were resistant to the technology, and we feared that a future might be built without their being part of the barn-raising of this new technological world order.

After "NFTs-WTF?," we got the band back together for a more extended and expanded exploration of the topic—the four-episode series "Putting the Fun in Non-Fungible Tokens," on which this book is based and which aired on MCA Denver's YouTube channel in the fall of 2021. We invited leading thinkers, artists, makers, scholars, and other fellow travelers to try to make sense of this rapidly evolving space. Our desire was not to defend or to persuade but instead to understand the shifting ground underneath our field and the ways in which the technology could completely reshape much more than the arts.

It may be easy and tempting to sit on the sidelines of NFTs, writing them off as a flash-in-the-pan market craze, or a degradation of the environment, or a bore, especially because of the tone in which NFTs are often described—a grandiose future and a messianic claim about being there at the beginning. While being allergic to that tone is relatable, there is something much more important and structural that has nothing to do with the market spectacle, the price of cryptocurrency, the feeling of a science-fiction future, or the inescapable clubbiness of the NFT space. We find the NFT phenomenon to be something very different from all of these: NFTs and blockchain—at their best—can be understood as a collaborative human project, much like art.

THE INVITATION TO THE BOOK

Rather than talk *around* NFTs—as art-world albatross and one-dimensional, commercial excess—we want to invite everyone, especially those of us without a Ph.D. in cryptography, to understand NFTs and to imagine the radical potential shifts in the power structure of the arts that may come about from this technology.

The purpose of the project has been to create an approachable and engaging but also rigorous and inquisitive primer on non-fungible tokens, based on speaking with people who were building things—the makers and artists of blockchain and NFTs. For our research, we engaged many different people who are making them, who are donating them to museums, and who are critiquing them, especially with regard to the environment and to equity for artists. Both the spring and fall 2021 programs are available to watch for free on MCA Denver's YouTube channel (and

1998
Founding
of Google

we encourage you to do so!), and they offer a foundation for—and a complement to—the ideas we explore more deeply in this publication.

From our first forays sketching the outline on a whiteboard at MCA Denver, the project always felt like a book. The book felt important, beyond the series, because it allows us to probe the subject more comprehensively, to synthesize ideas informed by the many voices in the program, and to take experimental conversations and distill them into this primer.

While the program allowed us a planned but spontaneous space of one hour—or a little more—each week for four weeks to build ideas, the book allows us more time and space to reflect and to develop the different stories of NFTs and to bring forward an even keener awareness of the larger democratic and societal import of the ideas we were discussing in a program about art. A book also felt like the right way to invite people into conversation—at the pace of reading and with the pleasures of the ways that especially books can invite us into stories. We also felt that no such publication existed in the arts that took as broad a view of the origins of the NFT phenomenon—from technology to democracy, artists' sustainability, and shifting power structures. As with any new technology, the NFT space is rapidly evolving, in relation to everything from cryptocurrency markets to artistic experimentation to regulation. What we want to do here is to tell the enduring parts of the story—the origins, its timeline to date, its key inventions, and its most important questions, skepticisms, and potential consequences.

15

THE BIG IDEAS OF THE BOOK

Blockchain is a new technology that is founded on established ideas in cryptography, the branch of computer science concerned with code-breaking or encryption of information using computing tools. Blockchain is, in the words of cryptographer and computer science professor Joseph Bonneau, "an append-only ledger" or "public bulletin board."[3] What that means is that blockchain gives us a record of information that can be public—verifiable by all—and which can be added to ("append-only") but never subtracted from. In addition, certain actions—like transfers of funds—can be set to happen automatically through so-called "smart" or self-executing contracts. Thus, the public ledger can also transparently record transactions, and these smart contracts can be put together into groups. Those groups of smart contracts operate like an organizational decision-making process, what is called a decentralized autonomous organization, or DAO. The public ledger, the ability to automate an action through a smart contract, and the ability to join up multiple smart contracts into DAOs create very new ways of relating to trust in information, oversight of decisions, and the way people come together to collaborate, contract, and design systems.

2000
U.S. Supreme Court decides *Bush v. Gore*,
making George W. Bush U.S. president

The crux of blockchain is a technological engagement with many philosophical questions about knowledge, trust, and truth. The epistemological problem—how we know what we know—is the motivation of blockchain as a system of publicly engineered trust in records that does not require trust in the record-keeper. Of course, creating immutable trust or truth is complicated, if not impossible, in a technology still populated by people. As a system, blockchain is not perfect; as the saying goes, garbage in, garbage out. In 2018 a man named Terence Eden famously listed himself on the company Verisart's blockchain as the creator of Leonardo da Vinci's *Mona Lisa* with 1506 as the production date. That record will always be on the Verisart blockchain.[4] Even if the information is inaccurate, it cannot be deleted, only added to as a correction or update to the information. What we do have is the knowledge that that record can never be deleted and that subsequent corrections cannot be deleted either. Blockchain is a structure of keeping information that is time-stamped and organized in cryptographically secured ways. This gives it both transparency and precision while instilling trust that the information, whether true or not, has not been altered. It affirms that the integrity of information has not been manipulated.

While this system is still human—and counterintuitively more organic than its technological machinery would make it seem—even a system based on such documentary aims as transparency and time-stamping can also create radical new forms of power, organization, collaboration, and trust. For these reasons alone, blockchain holds wild and exciting democratic possibility: it could radically change power structures in the art world and create new mechanisms by which artists are funded more sustainably, for example. Because it enables artists to sell their work directly and because many new buyers face few barriers to entering the NFT space, the technology could also disrupt some of the taste-making structures of the arts, from galleries and critics to museums.

A new cultural phenomenon that upends such traditional structures warrants scrutiny and discourse and is precisely the type of subject matter that organizations like MCA Denver seek to engage with because it reveals powerful narratives about our present moment. Beyond issues of taste or aesthetics, understanding why artists are turning to this technology and why some collectors are put off by it tells us something about our contemporary context that demands investigation. If artists can hold a mirror up to our reality and reflect it back to audiences through their work, then artists' engagement in pioneering the NFT phenomenon holds compelling lessons for us to decode.

Decoding these lessons in the arts also has something to teach us about the potential of blockchain to change the larger world. The possibility, but by no means the certainty, of blockchain has to do with democracy—with the building of self-governing systems that operate on the transparency of a public and immutable

2004
Founding
of Facebook

ledger, rather than with trust in a central authority such as a government. The implication of these changes is that power could shift away from the governments, institutions, and the large platform companies—Google or Facebook, to name two—that are so central to our economic and political systems. Thus, blockchain has enormous potential for both generative and positive futures and also risks causing structural instability in systems that may already be decaying but whose sturdiness we still take for granted.

The particular power—or destabilization or creative potential—of blockchain is its capacity to reorient power from centralized institutions to the public. As new areas such as artificial intelligence (AI) are centralizing—feeding data into an algorithm—blockchain is decentralizing—building an interconnected ledger in many copies. At the same time, blockchain is developing within existing power structures in which banks, technology companies, and the programmers of various blockchain technologies may have motivation to preserve or build re-centralizing power, however entrenched, brittle, or stale that existing institutional power may be.

We are writing this book and exploring blockchain at a time of eroded trust or faith in institutions. Facebook was founded in 2004. Twitter launched in 2006. The reality show *Keeping Up with the Kardashians* hit the airwaves in 2007 and illustrated how manipulated and fabricated "reality" can be. Then in 2010, the U.S. Supreme Court decided *Citizens United*, declaring corporations to be people and money as speech, which quickly flooded the U.S. government with special interest funds.[5] We are more than a decade into not really knowing how deeply vast amounts of money circulate in politics or the advertising policies of Facebook, nor the sources of that money. We could analyze these phenomena from 30,000 feet, but what they reveal most crucially is that we have fewer shared truths than we ever have. We don't agree on what is true. As Kevin McCoy, who made the first NFT (Fig. 1), said, "People will *die* for stories."[6]

This is where we arrive at this book's journey into and curiosity about NFTs and blockchain. At its core, blockchain originates from a concern with trust—how we know what was true about the past and how we know that without trusting a central authority to keep the record. That starting point, the origin of blockchain in a knowledge story, is not just a story of money or technology but also a mirror held up to the ways we understand ourselves and our history. The promise of trusting what we know—of securing truth, even—may seem idealistic, and the reality may be closer to transparency or simple records. Yet the architects of the proto-blockchain—Stuart Haber and Scott Stornetta, whom we meet in the next chapter—were grappling with how easy it was to alter a digital file without anyone being able to tell. Thus, the record and the time-stamped, cryptographically secure organization of the record they created offered a robust and, at the time, pioneering way of holding space for truth by calling out the doctoring of information of any kind.

2006
Founding
of Twitter

We fully acknowledge earned skepticism toward the technology—whether because of its fundamental attributes, its environmental impact, its occasional clubbiness, or the often ostentatious tone in which its future is championed. No matter what, NFTs sit squarely in the middle of one of the very biggest questions of our time: the relationship of capitalism and democracy. Watching the U.S. democracy become fragile in the post-truth age only adds to the speculation over blockchain's future. As we contemplate propagandistic arguments over critical race theory or unexamined and pervasive institutional and individual racism and histories of wealth disparity, NFTs offer unusual starting points for public recording of fact and related creative development of systems of redistribution, acknowledgment, and repair.

With these very big questions, the arts offer a sandbox to work out some ideas about value. For some, the arts may seem a limited arena in which to consider these questions. But for those who understand that art is a ground for joy, provocation, self-understanding, and the electric energy that human beings can create to push the frontiers of society or the endlessly large envelope of meaning in the everyday, it will be very clear. And while the arts remain intimately connected to questions of value, they also pose vital questions around perspective, agreement, vision, and imagination. How do we understand that, especially when we disagree? How do we make decisions together? Who gets resources? How do we parse the very newest things—dismissively or openly but rigorously—especially when the very newest things are often messy and imperfect? Do we extend them grace and curiosity or resist them? The arts are a microcosm for these larger questions of power, imagination, and creative possibility, and this book is an invitation to be part of the conversation.

This book is not only about blockchain, NFTs, and what they are, but also about orienting toward justice, creativity, and the reimagination of society. Blockchain stems from an obsession with what we know, how we know it is true, and whether we trust the record-keeper. Today it is even harder for all of us to agree on common truths, more than it ever has been. So maybe what we can agree on is to live with common questions. The arts and museums give us fertile ground on which to grapple with the trauma of colonial roots, ideas of the past that we can accept the invitation to reconsider, and imaginative possibilities for reconciliation that are not zero-sum—one winner and one loser—but instead generative.

2007
Reality show *Keeping Up
with the Kardashians* debuts

THE MAP OF THE BOOK

We have structured this book as a series of stories that intersect, overlap, and inform each other. To that end, we are moving both chronologically and circuitously to lay out the multitude of developments, connections, and bridges that emerge. We begin with origin stories (Chapter 1), which recount the history of what would become the blockchain and how it relates to the history of contemporary art. Looking at two focal points—one in the realm of technology and the other in conceptual art—allows us to demonstrate how distinctly they emerged and then how interwoven they become in shared concern for provenance, authenticity, and the complicated relationship of artistic or technological innovation to markets. Chapter 1 also includes a breakdown of the essential terms that define this phenomenon, to arm our readers with a clear understanding of what we will be exploring over the course of the book. Origin stories often emerge from profound questions about vexing or powerful themes, in this instance specifically related to questions around trust and truth. In this way, we introduce how the story of the blockchain, and its application across industries, becomes a story about creative production, ownership, and, ultimately, democracy.

Chapter 2, or artists' stories, grounds these larger ideas within the narrative of those who are making, creating, and advancing the technology as designers and artists. This chapter focuses on the application and use of blockchain and the development of NFTs—and the curiosity and ambition that ushered in a new medium with which artists could experiment. The creation of NFTs quickly invites questions of collecting, distributing, and displaying these digital works of art more broadly. Chapter 3, on collectors and buying, probes more deeply into the twin realities of parsing NFTs artistically and navigating the regulatory, technological, and other logistical contexts of acquiring and stewarding them. Bringing together diverse expertise on collecting, selling, securing, and distributing NFTs, this chapter considers not just the "how" of acquiring but also the "why" behind collectors' decision-making around ownership and the future of presenting NFTs, collection-building, and donating to museums.

After exploring the birth, the development, and the dispersal of NFTs within a contemporary art context, Chapter 4 proposes novel approaches for the application of blockchain in the future. In what ways might this technology upend existing power structures, while also initiating new systems based on transparency, equity, and, above all, trust—a fulfillment of the original concept that drove Haber and Stornetta's early time-stamping innovation? The possibilities offered by the technology and the creative minds experimenting with it may very well enable a whole new ecosystem to emerge that prioritizes openness, community, collaboration, and innovation as central to its strength and sustainability. We conclude the book

2008
Fall of Lehman Brothers and
start of global financial crisis

with a series of questions, rather than answers, to affirm the sheer newness of the possibilities that lie ahead. A sense of belief in and skepticism about this potential pose myriad questions about how and why we need to grapple with this technology for relevancy and opportunity.

This book draws on interviews with leading contributors to the NFT story, including Stuart Haber and Scott Stornetta; David Yermack, the chair of the finance department at New York University and an early researcher and teacher of digital currencies; Kevin McCoy, the artist and professor who in 2014 made the world's very first NFT; Beatriz Ramos and Judy Mam, the co-founders of the early collaborative drawing platform DADA that created the NFT collection *Creeps & Weirdos*; and a host of other art world actors and early collectors, including Eduardo Burillo, who donated a *CryptoPunk* to the ICA Miami so early that the museum encountered difficulties accepting the donation; Pablo Rodriguez-Fraile, founder of Aorist, a cultural institution in the immersive digital world known as the metaverse; and Cheryl Finley, inaugural director of the Atlanta University Center Art History + Curatorial Studies Collective, distinguished visiting professor, Spelman College, and associate professor, Cornell University, considering questions of equity and inclusion in the NFT space. We hope you take pleasure in this book, that you feel our curiosity, and that you join in the story and share your own thoughts and responses, with us and with each other.

Whatever comes of NFTs, we believe that they offer the promise of profound transformation of the arts, enough that everyone needs to be invited into the conversation in order to shape and mold it. Whether you are an art dealer, a museum curator, an artist working in any medium, an art worker, an art collector, an observer of the arts, or an otherwise interested generalist, we hope this book provides a hospitable, precise, and accessible introduction to the subject. The invitation is for all of us to engage with this developing future, not to dismiss it out of hand but to spend time, much as we might as an art historian with a work of art, in close looking—and, much as we would as an artist, in radical presence and attention to the messiness of the work itself.

2008
LeWitt retrospective
launches at MASS MoCA

Satoshi Nakamoto circulates Bitcoin white paper, building
a currency around Haber and Stornetta's time-stamping

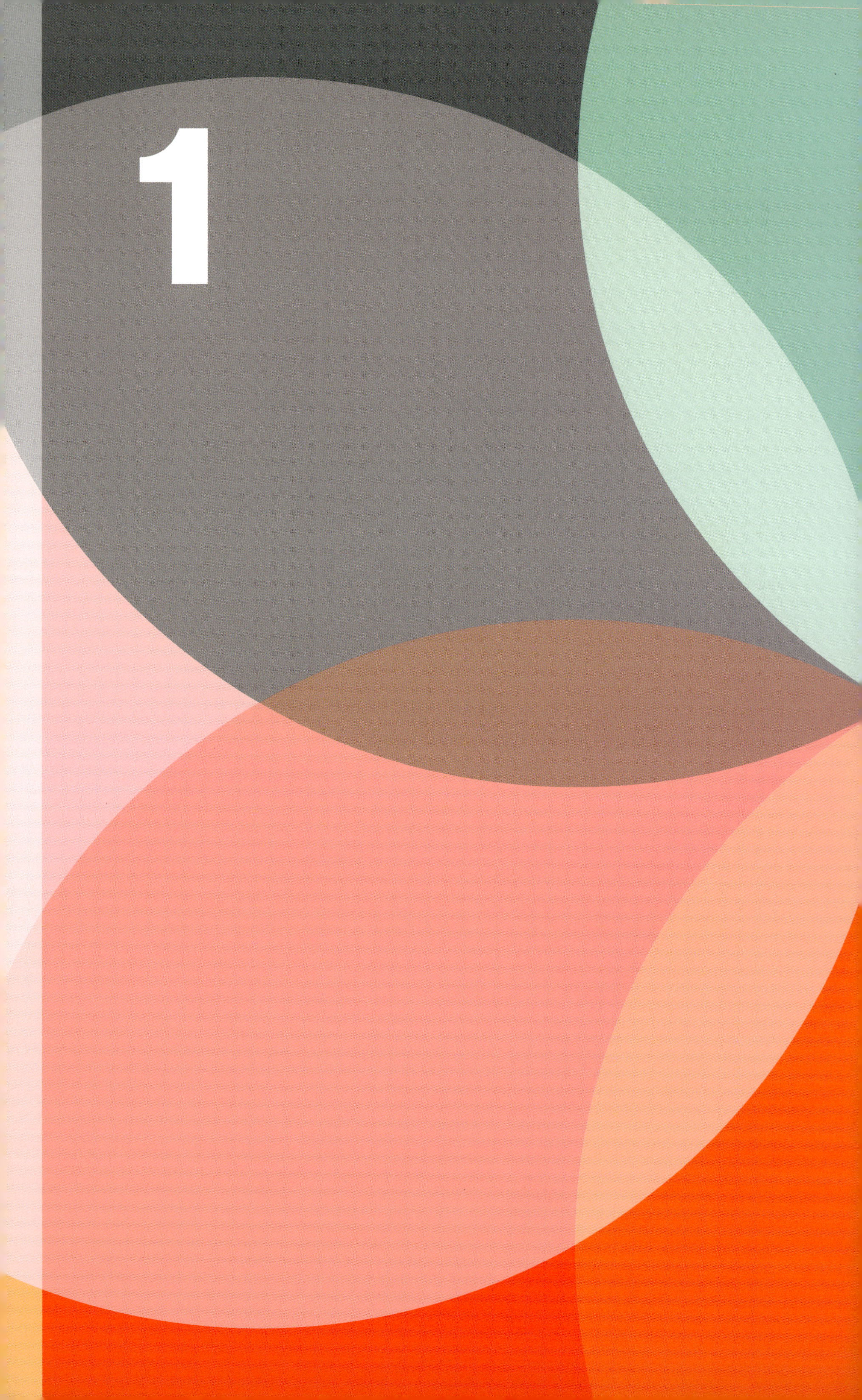
1

ORIGIN STORIES

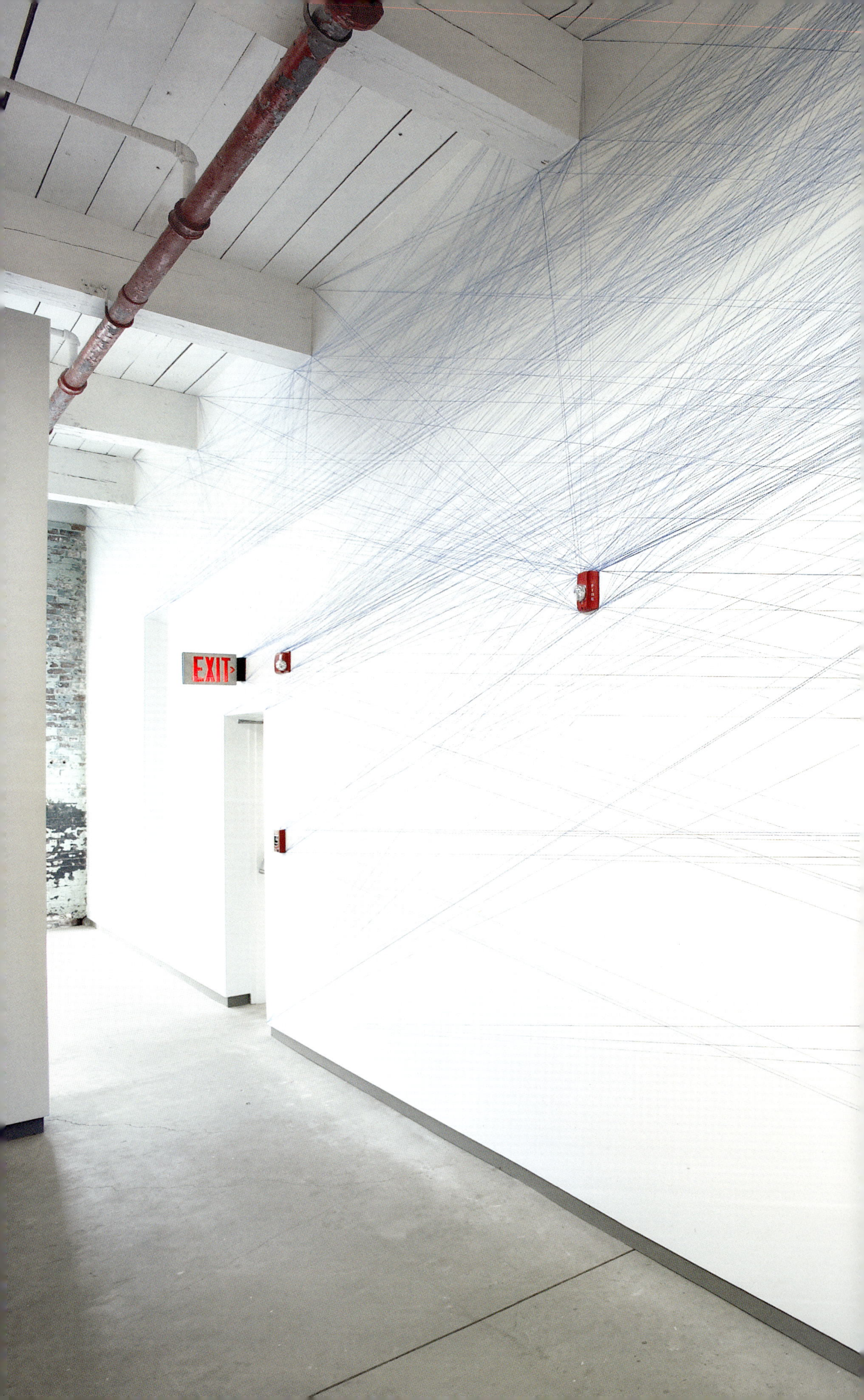

EXIT

You know, the notion of NFTs is pretty simple. It's just using a blockchain to track ownership of a digital object. It's one of the simplest applications of the smart contract. So, all the technical properties are very easy to ensure. I think the difficulty is what the real world meaning of an NFT is, which is a place where cryptographers can't really help you.

—JOSEPH BONNEAU, CRYPTOGRAPHER AND COMPUTER SCIENCE PROFESSOR

IN AUTUMN 2008, JUST AFTER the fall of Lehman Brothers and the precipitation of the global financial crisis, Satoshi Nakamoto—who is a person, or a group of people, or a pseudonym, and this is intentionally vague—began circulating a white paper proposing "Bitcoin," a cryptocurrency, meaning a form of money backed by cryptographic tools, as opposed to "fiat" money, backed by governments. The idea of a money system outside of government was inseparable from both the longtime crypto-anarchist histories of resistance to government and market control and the seismic precarity sweeping global financial systems.

Market critique and resistance also have a long history in the arts. Notably, the conceptual artist Sol LeWitt began making wall drawings in 1968, explicitly

Fig. 1 *(opposite and following pages)* Sol LeWitt, *Wall Drawing 51*. All architectural points connected by straight lines, June 1970. Installation view, MASS MoCA, North Adams, MA, ongoing.

2009
Satoshi Nakamoto launches
Bitcoin blockchain

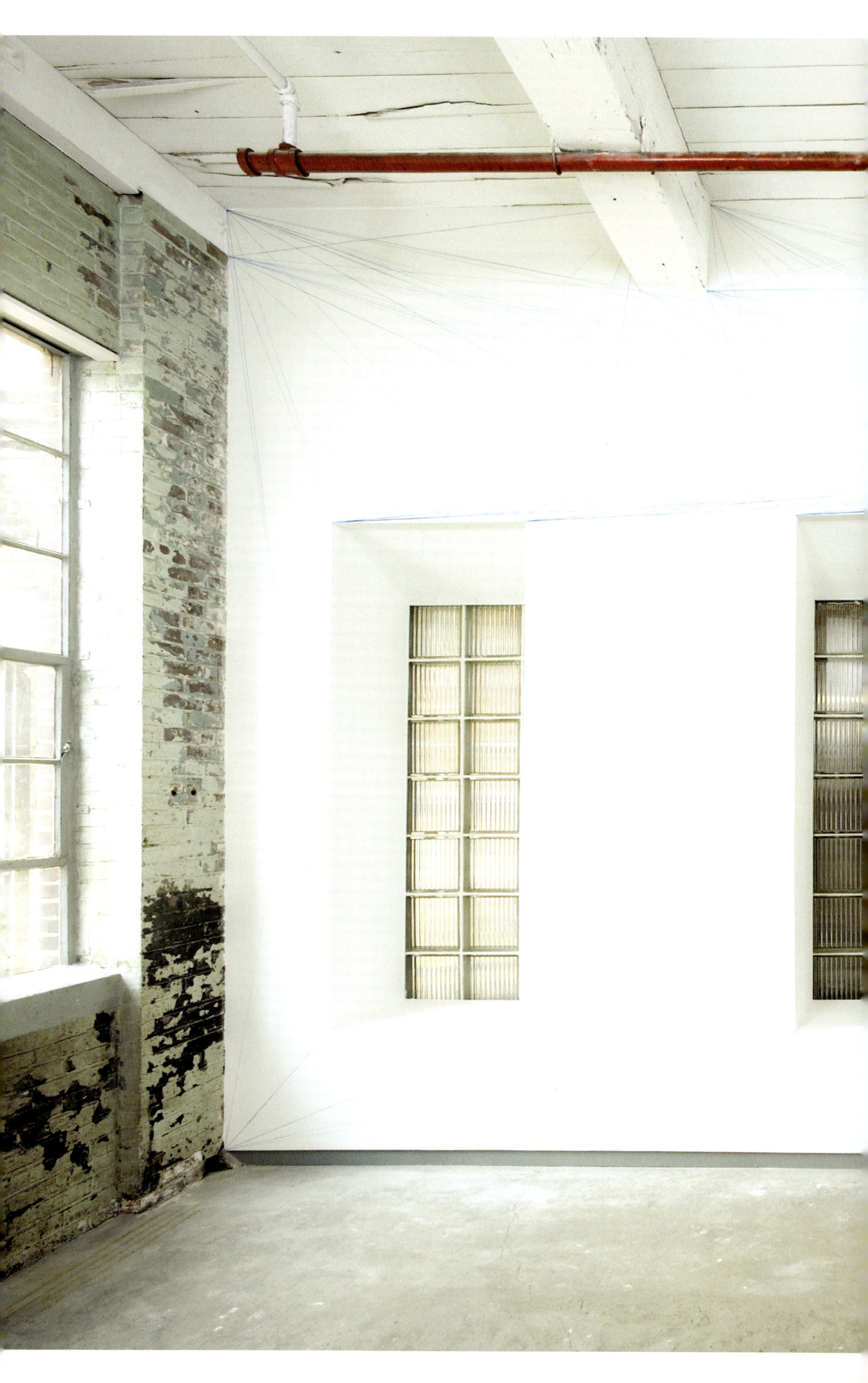

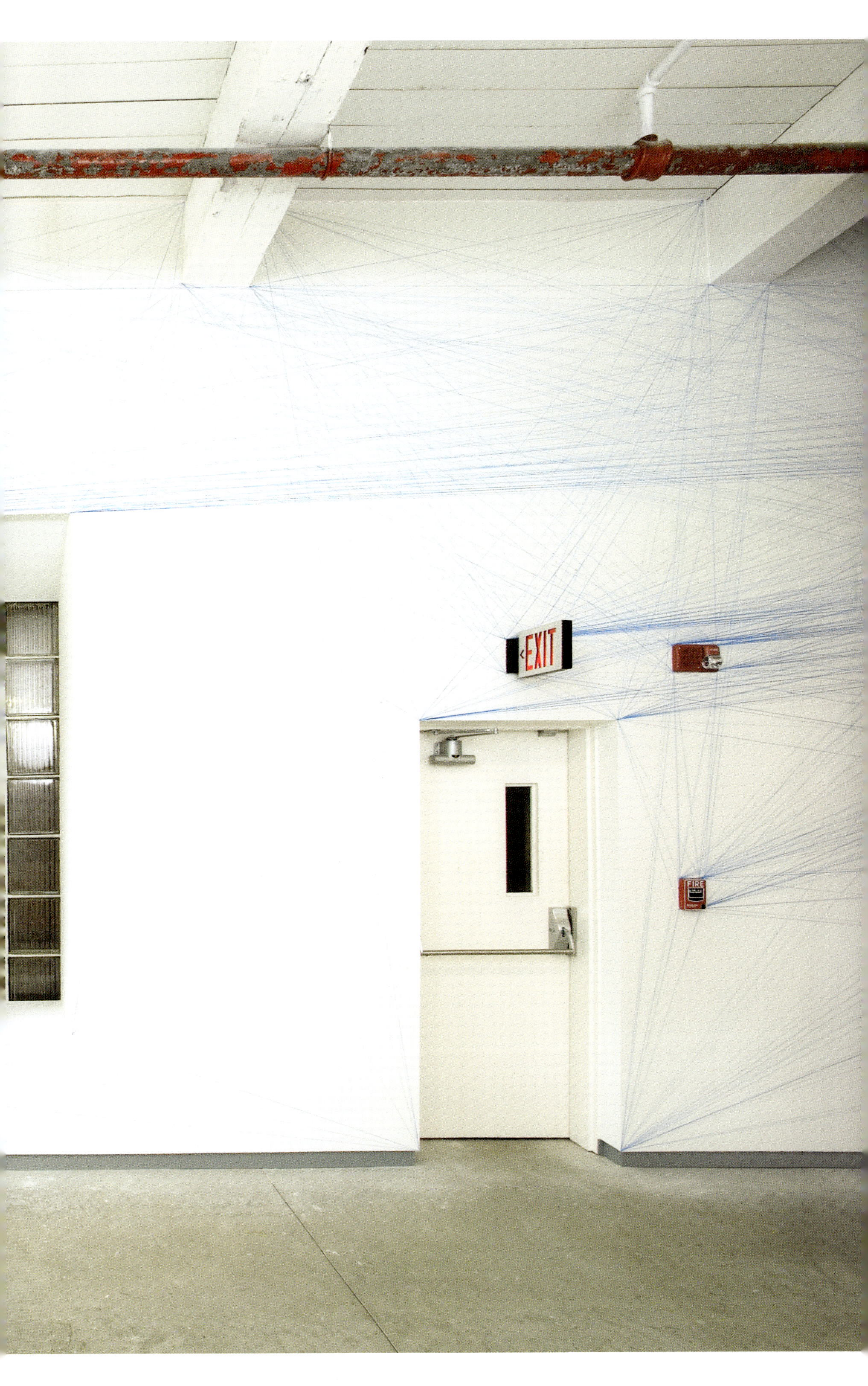

EXIT
FIRE

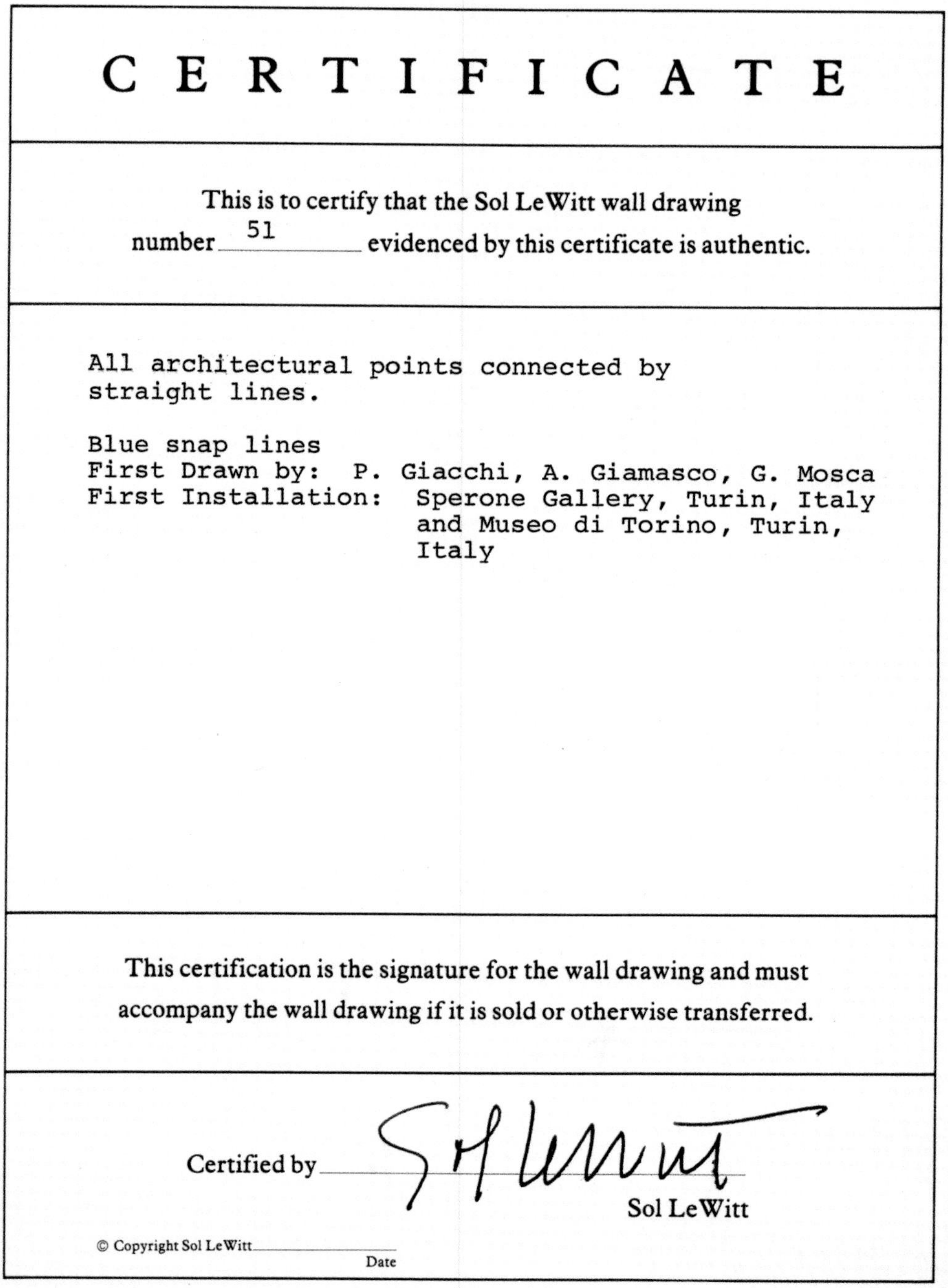

C E R T I F I C A T E

This is to certify that the Sol LeWitt wall drawing
number _____51_____ evidenced by this certificate is authentic.

```
All architectural points connected by
straight lines.

Blue snap lines
First Drawn by:  P. Giacchi, A. Giamasco, G. Mosca
First Installation:  Sperone Gallery, Turin, Italy
                     and Museo di Torino, Turin,
                     Italy
```

This certification is the signature for the wall drawing and must

accompany the wall drawing if it is sold or otherwise transferred.

Certified by ________________________________

Sol LeWitt

© Copyright Sol LeWitt __________________
Date

Fig. 2
Sol LeWitt,
Certificate of
Authenticity,
*Wall Drawing
51*, undated.

DIAGRAM

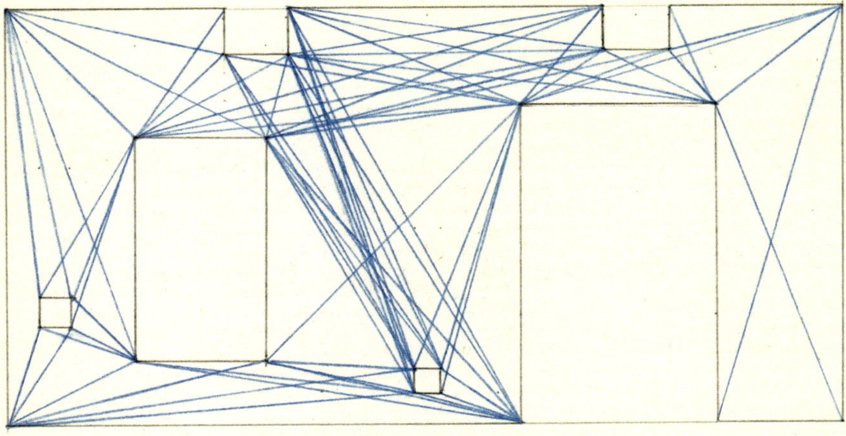

This is a diagram for the Sol LeWitt wall drawing number __*51*__ . It should accompany the certificate if the wall drawing is sold or otherwise transferred but is not a certificate or a drawing.

Fig. 3
Sol LeWitt,
Wall Drawing
51, Diagram,
Wall Drawing
51, undated.

to avoid making salable paintings on canvas. The concept or idea of the work *was* the work, and it was codified in a certificate of authenticity that declared the idea to be LeWitt's (Figs. 2 and 3). Although LeWitt's work has been lionized by the art world for decades, a singular honoring of his work took place at the same time that the Bitcoin white paper was circulating in fall 2008. The Massachusetts Museum of Contemporary Art (MASS MoCA) opened a twenty-five-year-long retrospective of LeWitt's wall drawings, including 105 examples made between 1969 and 2007, providing the most in-depth and long-term study of the artist's conceptual practice to date (Fig. 1).

Satoshi's proposal to build a system that operated outside of existing power structures of markets and governments echoes and engages with this much longer history of market resistance from within the visual arts, especially LeWitt's landmark engineering of a type of art-making that evaded commercial systems. In their own distinct though rigorously innovative ways, LeWitt and Satoshi ushered in market-resistant forms that changed how we think about authenticity, property, and registration through certificates of authenticity—or non-fungible tokens on the blockchain. However, like Bitcoin, market-resistant art would later become subsumed by the very markets it was trying to avoid.

In his 1967 "Paragraphs on Conceptual Art" LeWitt famously wrote, "The idea becomes a machine that makes the art."[7] The wall drawings were sets of instructions, and the instructions were the art. The drawings were then executed, initially by the artist himself and then by skilled artisans whom the artist trained. Figure 1 shows *Wall Drawing 51,* first executed in June 1970 in Italy, for which the instructions are "All architectural points connected by straight lines."

As Chris Vacchio, the director of research for the LeWitt catalogue raisonné, told us, when LeWitt first started making wall drawings—at Paula Cooper Gallery in 1968—it was "essentially about the idea of putting the work directly on the


```
00000000  01 00 00 00 00 00 00 00   00 00 00 00 00 00 00 00   ................
00000010  00 00 00 00 00 00 00 00   00 00 00 00 00 00 00 00   ................
00000020  00 00 00 00 3B A3 ED FD   7A 7B 12 B2 7A C7 2C 3E   ....;£íýz{.²zÇ,>
00000030  67 76 8F 61 7F C8 1B C3   88 8A 51 32 3A 9F B8 AA   gv.a.È.Ã^ŠQ2:Ÿ,ª
00000040  4B 1E 5E 4A 29 AB 5F 49   FF FF 00 1D 1D AC 2B 7C   K.^J)«_Iÿÿ...¬+|
00000050  01 01 00 00 00 01 00 00   00 00 00 00 00 00 00 00   ................
00000060  00 00 00 00 00 00 00 00   00 00 00 00 00 00 00 00   ................
00000070  00 00 00 00 00 00 FF FF   FF FF 4D 04 FF FF 00 1D   ......ÿÿÿÿM.ÿÿ..
00000080  01 04 45 54 68 65 20 54   69 6D 65 73 20 30 33 2F   ..EThe Times 03/
00000090  4A 61 6E 2F 32 30 30 39   20 43 68 61 6E 63 65 6C   Jan/2009 Chancel
000000A0  6C 6F 72 20 6F 6E 20 62   72 69 6E 6B 20 6F 66 20   lor on brink of
000000B0  73 65 63 6F 6E 64 20 62   61 69 6C 6F 75 74 20 66   second bailout f
000000C0  6F 72 20 62 61 6E 6B 73   FF FF FF FF 01 00 F2 05   or banksÿÿÿÿ..ò.
000000D0  2A 01 00 00 00 43 41 04   67 8A FD B0 FE 55 48 27   *....CA.gŠý°þUH'
000000E0  19 67 F1 A6 71 30 B7 10   5C D6 A8 28 E0 39 09 A6   .gñ¦q0·.\Ö¨(à9.¦
000000F0  79 62 E0 EA 1F 61 DE B6   49 F6 BC 3F 4C EF 38 C4   ybàê.aÞ¶Iö¼?Lï8Ä
00000100  F3 55 04 E5 1E C1 12 DE   5C 38 4D F7 BA 0B 8D 57   óU.å.Á.Þ\8M÷º..W
00000110  8A 4C 70 2B 6B F1 1D 5F   AC 00 00 00 00            ŠLp+kñ._¬....
```


2010

U.S. Supreme Court decides *Citizens United v. Federal Election Commission*

wall," not on a canvas hung on the wall. LeWitt's first drawing was sold based on the labor—the time it took to execute it.[8] His work was not made for the market in a traditional sense, but, over time, the artist developed a system of certifying the authenticity of his drawings—with these certificates emerging organically from sets of instructions, sometimes with a signature or a drawn diagram. The crux of the work was that the certificate conveying the instructions and authenticity—the idea—*was* the work, not the executed drawing. If a person who had a wall drawing executed in their home or institution then sold the certificate, that wall drawing ceased to be a LeWitt. The image and the ownership of it became untethered—much as would later happen with many NFTs.

Following the circulation of the Bitcoin white paper in fall 2008, the Bitcoin blockchain itself was launched January 3, 2009. The paper spoke to imaginative and political interests in systems of money and power outside of government control. It also proposed the cryptocurrency Bitcoin around a public registry of information. Satoshi—in the manner of Madonna or Cher—chose as the starting point—or genesis block—a headline from the *Times* of London, "Chancellor on Brink of Second Bailout for Bank," in the wake of the financial crisis (Fig. 4).

A blockchain is a database structure in which pieces of information are cryptographically connected together so that any change to that information is apparent. Cryptographically, any information added to a blockchain is put through a mathematical formula called a one-way hash function, a process that is almost impossible to reverse but that still allows you to verify the inputs. The hashed records are chained together with the summary hash from one block included in the next, not unlike a chain-link fence.

Satoshi's breakthrough invention was to create an incentive structure for many people to keep copies of and verify the sanctity of the distributed, shared ledger—the append-only bulletin board—of blockchain. Satoshi did this by creating the cryptocurrency Bitcoin. Those "miners" who solved cryptographic puzzles to verify the blocks of transactions—where a transaction can be the recording of any kind of information, not only a sale—won Bitcoin. In this way, cryptocurrency is the tail wagging the dog; the incentive to keep the ledger is a mechanism of maintenance, not the original purpose of the system.

The crux of NFTs is that blockchain allows a digital file—something that would be infinitely replicable—to be given a unique identifier. What we call an NFT is a way of creating a unique record of ownership on the blockchain. In this sense, a Sol LeWitt certificate of authenticity is very much like an NFT. It is not the work itself but the registration of the work that certifies it as the original artwork. Many people could have the drawing on their wall, but only one would own the LeWitt: the person with the certificate of authenticity.

Fig. 4
Satoshi Nakamoto, *Genesis Block*, January 3, 2009. Bitcoin blockchain.

2010
Bitcoin
Pizza Day

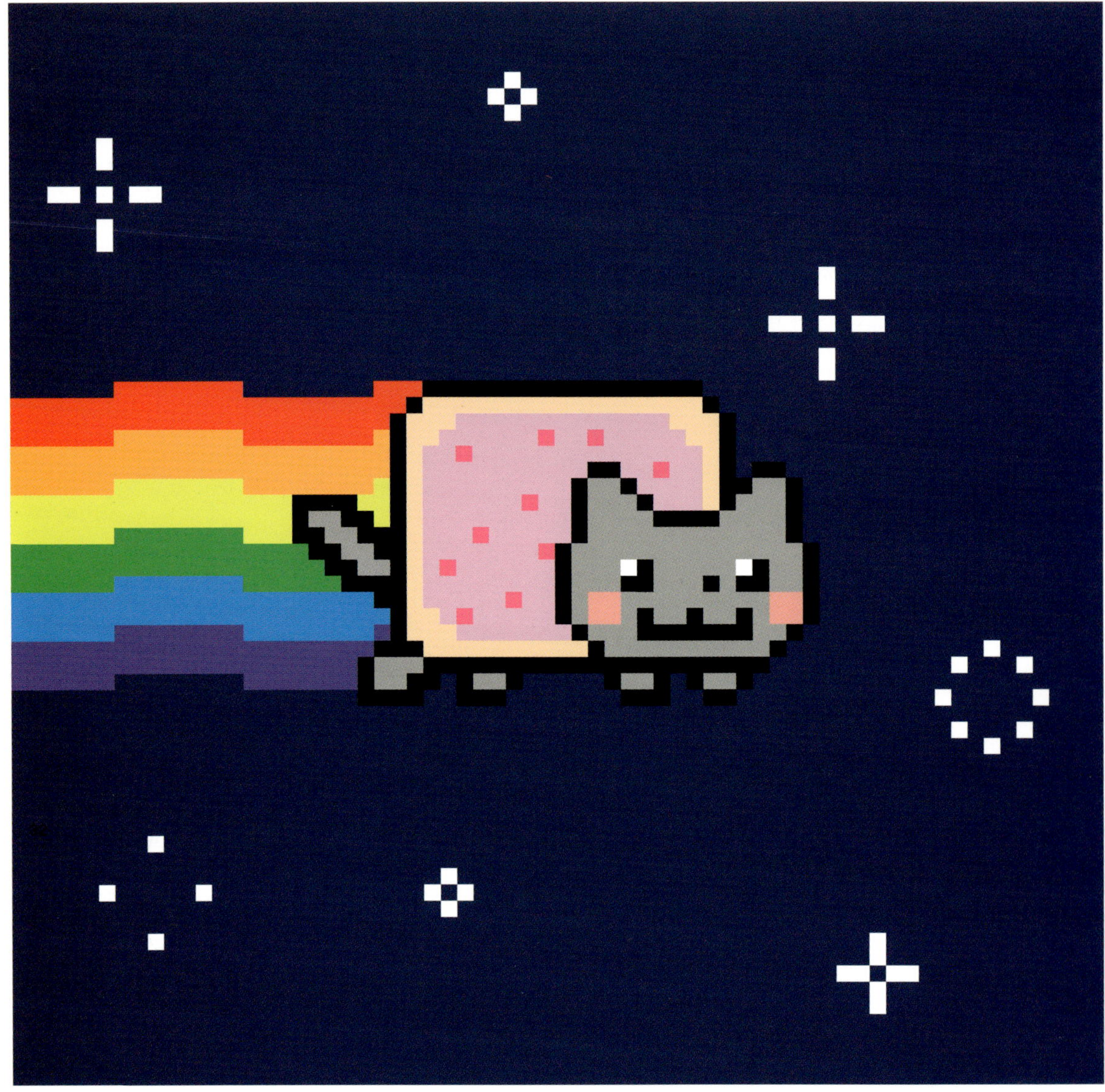

As mentioned in the introduction, the landmark NFT sale in March 2021 of Mike Winkelmann's *Everydays: The First 5000 Days* for more than 69 million dollars launched NFTs into the popular discourse and forever changed the conversation around them in the art world. Without in any way discounting the criticisms of the work, it brought to the fore a conversation about works like it—that is, digital artworks that are structured like a LeWitt. Anyone can download a copy of Beeple's high resolution file from the Internet, but only one person owns the NFT or the right to sell it.

The sale price of Beeple's NFT made parsing the value of art even more confusing than usual. The month before, *Nyan Cat* (Fig. 5), a meme that had been in circulation since 2011, sold for 300 ETH (the cryptocurrency associated with the Ethereum blockchain), then equivalent to around 690,000 dollars.

Some of these sales went beyond jaw-dropping prices; they also started to upend institutional structures within the arts. When Beeple's *Everydays* sold at Christie's, 91 percent of the bidders were new to the auction house.[9] Many NFTs were sold directly by artists without going through the taste-making or vetting systems of the arts—critics, curators, dealers. To make sense of these changes brought by NFTs, we identified a set of intersecting stories—some about art and artists, others about money and technology, and the most poignant yet overlooked ones about knowledge and democracy.

THE INTERSECTING STORIES OF BLOCKCHAIN

While much of the public imagination centers a money story or a technology story, we focus, too, on artists' stories, democracy stories, and—in the foundations of blockchain, the technology underneath NFTs—a knowledge story that has many affinities with the idea of provenance, that is, the history of an artwork's ownership (see Fig. 6, which is color-coded to the left margin throughout this book).

THE KNOWLEDGE STORY

The prequel to the Satoshi paper and all that has followed it is the work of two scientists—a cryptographer named Stuart Haber and a physicist named Scott Stornetta—who built the time-stamping system underneath blockchain not because they were in any way interested in cryptocurrency but because they cared about truth. Other scientists in this area notably include Ralph Merkle, the inventor of the Merkle tree, an elegant way to unforgeably and efficiently summarize a long list of information items into a single concise hash value or digital fingerprint that can represent the entire list of items. As Bonneau told us, "If you have a thousand transactions in a Bitcoin block, they're represented by just one value, which is the root of a Merkle tree computed on all of the transactions in the block."

While the Merkle tree is critical, it is the time-stamping contributions of Haber and Stornetta, and a third co-author of one paper, David Bayer, that built the foundational layer of Satoshi's system. Haber's and Stornetta's work accounts for three of the eight total footnotes in the 2008 Bitcoin white paper, including one of their papers with a third author, Bayer. Their work is a much overlooked knowledge story. In fact, this obsession with knowledge is fundamental. It also echoes the devotional process of asserting ownership, provenance, and authenticity. And it starts with one key question:

Fig. 5
Chris Torres,
Nyan Cat,
2021. Still from
animated GIF.

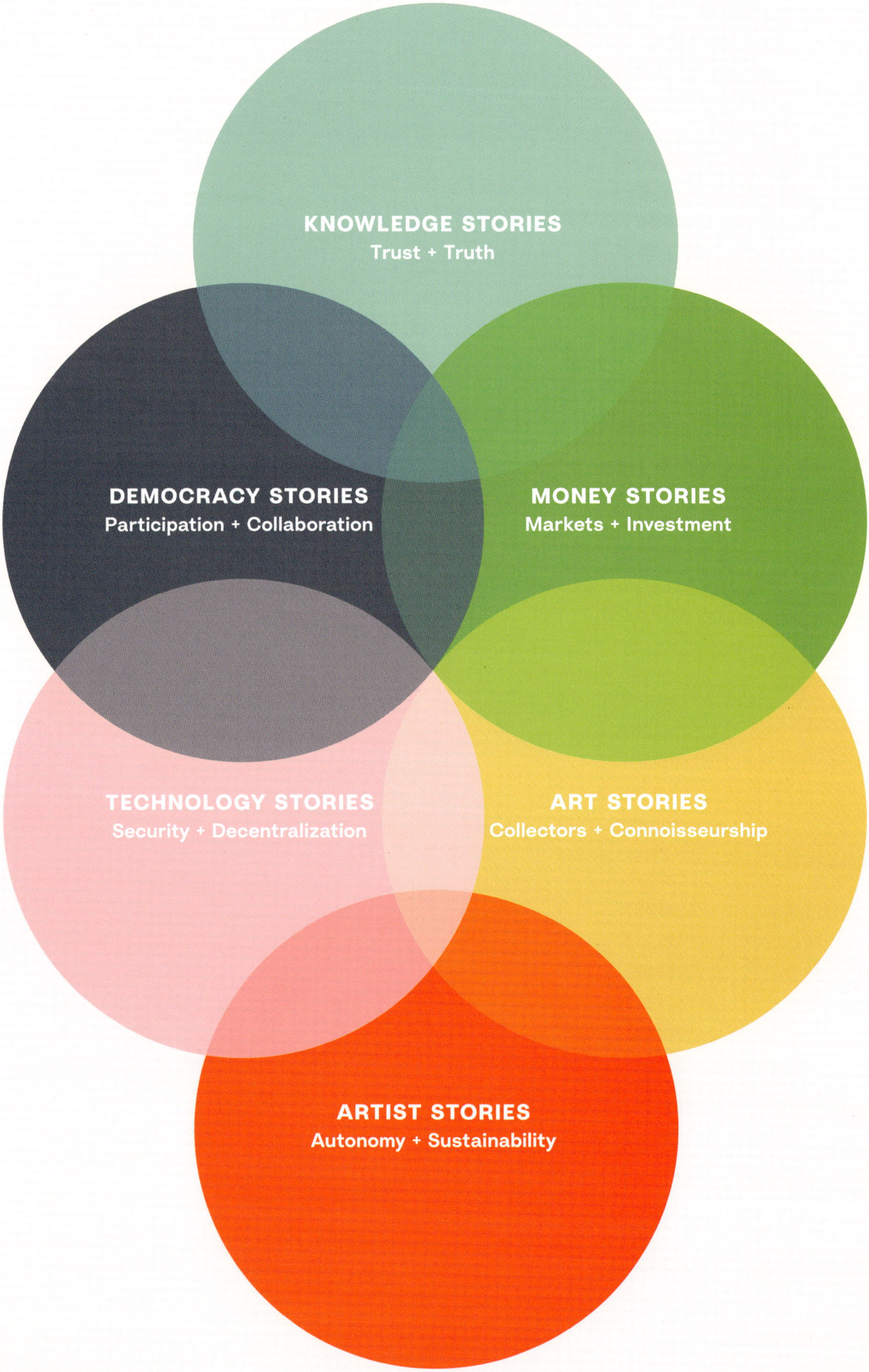

KNOWLEDGE STORIES
Trust + Truth

DEMOCRACY STORIES
Participation + Collaboration

MONEY STORIES
Markets + Investment

TECHNOLOGY STORIES
Security + Decentralization

ART STORIES
Collectors + Connoisseurship

ARTIST STORIES
Autonomy + Sustainability

How will we know what was true about the past without having to trust a central administrator to keep the record?

Haber and Stornetta met in the spring of 1989 when both were working at Bellcore—the think-tank-like research lab associated with the spin-out of the "Baby Bells" in the break-up of the phone company monopoly (with the larger "Ma Bell" associated with the storied research institution Bell Labs). Haber had interviewed Stornetta, and so a few weeks into his new job, Stornetta––who had relocated to the East Coast from his Ph.D. program at Stanford—approached inveterate New Yorker Haber with a research problem. At the time, personal computers were coming online. Especially to people like Haber and Stornetta, it had become painfully clear how easy it was to manipulate a digital file and how hard it would be to know if someone had done so.

They tried to design a system in which digital information—any information—could be trusted via a digital time-stamp, but they were stumped: Without the central administrator, how could you prevent cheaters? One day Stornetta and his family were at a Friendly's Restaurant in Morristown, New Jersey, waiting (by the ice cream cakes) for a table when Stornetta had a breakthrough. If adding one more person always added a cheater, then if you added everyone the problem went away. Inverting the problem gave them a solution. Stornetta's wife, Marcia, recalled that he went to bed that night saying he knew something no one else in the world did, except that he would not be sure it was true until he talked with Haber about it the next day.

The two worked out the problem and conceived of a system to time-stamp digital documents. The unassuming Haber presented it at Crypto '90, the punk-sounding but rather academic gathering of cryptographers in Santa Barbara, California. Apparently, even in the room Haber could feel from the energy that they had introduced a big idea. The plate tectonics that would later shift the art ecosystem were starting to nudge and slide among the researchers gathered. The official academic paper—the first of three—was published the following year, 1991, in the *Journal of Cryptology*.[10] For a paper introducing what may seem an arcane computing problem, the examples had a quiet liberal arts flair. Blockchain can register any kind of information—a picture of a cat on the Internet, the entire works of Marcel Proust. In their paper, they used the example of "Who will guard the guards?"—the Juvenal quotation, in the original Latin—and quoted from Shakespeare's *Lucrece* on the passage of time.

The idea of time-stamping digital documents seemed so exciting that Haber and Stornetta negotiated to spin out a company from Bellcore. Called Surety, the company could time-stamp any information. The most concrete use case was the time-stamping of laboratory notebooks—ones that had previously been held together

35

Fig. 6

The Intersecting Stories of Blockchain.

The advertisement image reproduced as text:

**NOTICES &
LOST AND
FOUND**
(5100–5102)

Universal Registry Entries:
Zone 2—
kSJISJLeqWNTttgPbDISHTlca
KWykvB/y3+4Jvqw3rokbBq
LHjV4YzrSqJp5jgEy6lOfPQ==
Zone 3—
jZZAaRRr2wRcZqDlkAyN1p
zHZUZF1wX4x03njt/1qochEQCB
Xuqxwk4XYaglw9iFCSPGTQ==
Zone 4—
KQVnRLFYSxX17jfO227h/Ouh
Fx/M6vpg4ETGpUhGhRMnAT
bDHEJGx9HUQ3Abji92dO+aEg==
These base64-encoded values repre-
sent the combined fingerprints of all
digital records notarized by Surety be-
tween 20220504Z - 20220510Z.
www.surety.com   239-436-2790

Fig. 7 *(right)*
Surety advertisement, *New York Times*, 2022. Courtesy of Drs. Stuart Haber and Scott Stornetta.

Fig. 8 *(opposite)*
Stuart Haber and Scott Stornetta in the *Star-Ledger*, November 20, 1990.

36

with a stitched binding and signed on each page by a supervisor. Now a digital service could ensure that no scientist had tampered with previous results.

As it turned out, Surety did not take off. In an alternate universe, we might have seen their time-stamping pulled into the infrastructure layer of computing, where most of us might check, say, a Microsoft Word file to see the date last modified. Although the firm was not commercially successful, with Haber and Stornetta joining the ranks of many artists who were ahead of their time, the Surety project did launch one long-standing conceptual artwork. Each Sunday, Surety would publish a different alphanumeric code in *The New York Times* (Fig. 7). The ads allowed Surety customers to confirm that no one had tampered with the time-stamping system and its data. The series of classified ads, still published, is the oldest blockchain in the world. The *Times* ad turned thirty in October 2021.

The problems Haber and Stornetta were grappling with are still here today and are taken for granted in some art-world use cases for blockchain. Their time-stamping system essentially answered a registrarial problem of provenance of the history of ownership of an artwork. This knowledge story would take on many lives and applications—from restitution of cultural objects to digital provenance for artists selling work now, to records of resale royalties paid to artists.

2014
DADA
launches

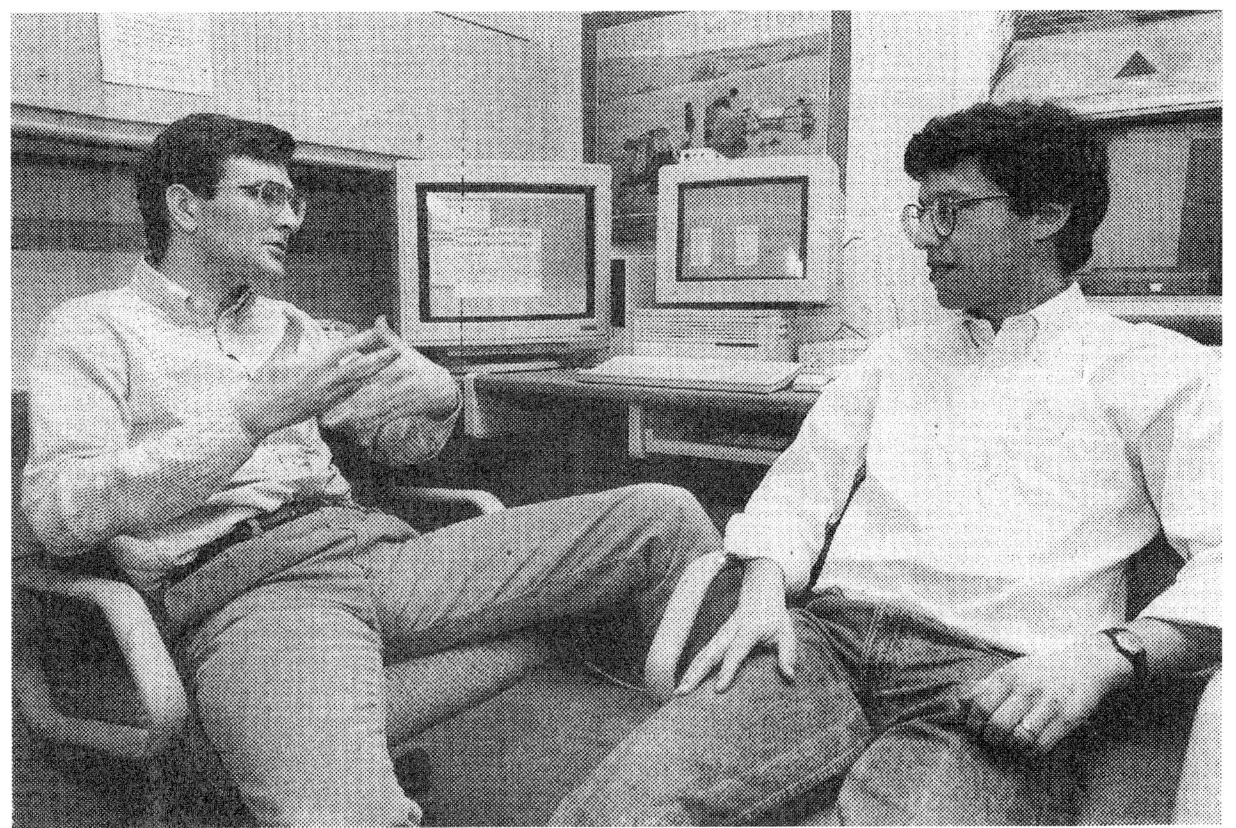

The knowledge story is still fallible and human, of course. In the early days of the press coverage, a New Jersey newspaper, the *Star-Ledger,* featured Haber and Stornetta (Fig. 8). They were mislabeled in the caption. Stornetta is actually on the left and Haber on the right, a fitting reminder that immutable records can contain human errors.

THE TECHNOLOGY STORY

Blockchain is often presented—logically so—as a technology story, because it is a specific and sophisticated combination of various tools from cryptography and math. (See the Appendix for more details.)

When we talk about blockchain, we are speaking about the protocol, meaning the type of bulletin board, as it were. (A blockchain could also be said to be a virtual computer that creates this bulletin board.) We also talk about platforms (e.g., SuperRare, OpenSea), which are the digital storefronts through which we might access NFTs or manage other blockchain-registered works. A key distinction in blockchain protocols is the mechanism by which they create trust in the information. For instance, the Bitcoin blockchain uses Proof of Work

2015
Vitalik Buterin launches
Ethereum blockchain

(PoW), in which computers all over the world can compete using brute computing strength to find solutions to mathematical puzzles. As more Bitcoin goes into circulation, the energy consumption to solve these puzzles goes up exponentially. The Cambridge Bitcoin Electricity Consumption Index tracks the environmental impact of blockchain. In May 2022, Bitcoin's energy consumption was 117 terrawatt hours per year, falling between the annual consumption of the Netherlands (111 TWH/year) and Argentina (121.8 TWH/year). This consumption varies substantially with the price of Bitcoin, as a lower price disincentivizes miners from solving the brute-force puzzles.[11]

Another main blockchain protocol is Ethereum (Fig. 9), which was proposed in 2014 and launched in 2015 by Vitalik Buterin and collaborators. Ethereum was designed to be modular and relatively easier to program. The modular programming units are "tokens." A token is the data that registers an object such as an artwork. The token is governed by a smart contract, following from a token standard, such as the ERC-721 programming standard on the Ethereum blockchain. It was proposed in 2017 and implemented in early 2018. "ERC" stands for "Ethereum Request for Comments," the process by which programming

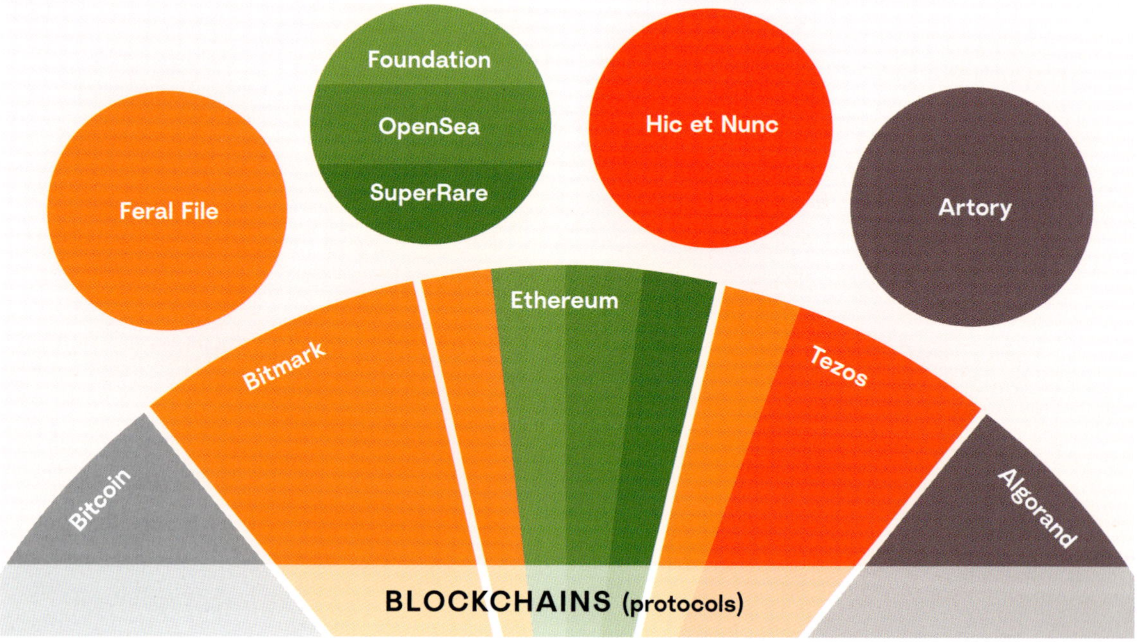

2017
Larva Labs (Matt Hall and John
Watkinson) launch *CryptoPunks*

standards are proposed, evaluated by the community, and formalized. (The earlier fungible token is the ERC-20, implemented in 2015.)

Like Bitcoin, Ethereum also uses the energy-consuming Proof of Work, though it has announced an intention to move to Proof of Stake (PoS). Proof of Stake uses a different system of anteing up cryptocurrency in order to transact and risking losing money through bad-faith action. The mechanism can be viewed a bit more like a lottery than PoW's competition to finish the puzzle first. The energy consumption of PoS goes up more linearly, thus drawing less environmental criticism.

We note that the environmental criticism is not as simple as it may seem. It goes without saying that the climate crisis extends far beyond cryptocurrency and at scales far more extreme. As David Yermack, a longtime blockchain researcher and chair of the finance department at New York University's Stern School of Business, notes, there are many tools in economics—such as "pricing in" pollution—that could solve for these problems, but some engagement with market tools, not just market criticism, would be required. As we discuss specifically in Chapter 4, Whitaker's research considers similar economically engaged methods that would provide economic proceeds to artists. The technology story is actually an interdisciplinary and even poetic entry point to blockchain. First, the machinelike nature of the technological trust machine actually requires organic maintenance, much as a gardener might prune trees and replant seeds. And second, the technology also requires holistic consideration—of economic, ethical, artistic, and other ways of thinking, especially all the ways in which trust among human beings is still central to the story.

THE MONEY STORY

Many people foreground the money story of cryptocurrencies even though in the Haber and Stornetta case, cryptocurrencies played a secondary role of incentivizing transactions. In addition, Bitcoin and other early cryptocurrencies did, in fact, come about through an interest in money, specifically a crypto-anarchist motivation to create systems of money outside government oversight. That is not to say the purpose was to fund illicit transactions such as drug trade—though that did happen in some early instances in the history of cryptocurrencies—so much as to allow autonomy, self-efficacy, and independence from governmental oversight. As Finn Brunton, a professor of science and technology studies at University of California Davis argues in *Digital Cash,* early cryptocurrencies were also idealistic, even utopian attempts to use money to design a world order outside of the current "normal" systems that were seen as crumbling. As Brunton described it, we generally lack the ability to fully imagine the future. Sometimes we are helped by fictions or science fictions, but our

Fig. 9
Platforms and
Protocols.

2017
Dapper Labs launches
CryptoKitties

money system is based on an assumption that the future will continue along our pre-existing, "ordinary" trajectory. Early experiments in cryptocurrency stemmed instead from a belief that our society and infrastructure of money were veering toward collapse. He points to how the underlying technology of this money story interrogates the structures of capitalism and also those of democracy and, therefore, might provide a way of designing a more utopian society.[12]

In practice, the early money story of Bitcoin was somewhat academic, as the theory-into-practice hurdle proved tall. Sean Moss-Pultz, the founder of Bitmark, remembered thinking of it as "nerd money." Then famously on May 22, 2010—about fifteen months after Satoshi launched the Bitcoin blockchain—a programmer named Laszlo Hanyecz tried to make Bitcoin "real" by involving it in a transaction. He offered to pay 10,000 bitcoins for someone to have two Papa John's pizzas delivered to his house—at a cost of about 30 dollars. The event became famous—and is still celebrated on Bitcoin Pizza Day because the amount of 10,000 bitcoins has grown to tens or hundreds of millions of dollars. For instance, when Bitcoin topped 65,000 dollars in November 2021, those pizzas had been bought for 650,000,000 dollars. As we will see, the ability to price a cryptocurrency—for price to equal value—is complicated in ways that are uncannily similar to how hard it is for price to represent the value of art. Still, this money story endures and is conflated with the money stories that circulate around art: that is, the celebration of marquee prices—with none more random, surprising, and iconic than Beeple's 69-million-dollar sale of the NFT *Everydays* in March 2021.

THE DEMOCRACY STORY

An overlooked story that is perhaps central to NFTs is what we call the democracy story. NFTs can be sold on blockchain by "smart" or self-executing contracts. In addition, groups of self-executing contracts can be joined together to create DAOs, or decentralized autonomous organizations. These contracts, their designers, the coders of different blockchain protocols, and the authors of the terms of service of different platforms are all engaged in a key activity of establishing systems of governance.

Here, the case of Vitalik Buterin, the founder of Ethereum, is particularly illustrative. In the spring of 2018, *Tank Magazine* published excerpts from an interview with Buterin by the curator Hans Ulrich Obrist (Fig. 10), the artistic director of the Serpentine Galleries in London, who is famous for having conducted interviews of artists since his teenage years.[13] The interview was printed in *Tank*, and Obrist gave us permission to watch the raw footage. Buterin said something really important and critical to the nature of governance. He compared himself to Mark Zuckerberg, the Facebook (now Meta) founder, and he said that the difference

2018
ERC-721 formalized by
Ethereum consortium

We find ourselves in an incredible moment where the boundaries of technology are increasingly intertwined with the foundations of society, government, culture and even identity. Still, technology is too treated as if it were an object in the corner, rather than the ever-present layer of much of the world's daily lives. Blockchain technology is even more challenging: at once exhilarating and unknowable to many with its rollercoaster volatility, seemingly endless promise and frustrating resistance to the easy explanation of what technology is and how it works.

Culture has never been more in need of the shot in the arm that blockchain represents; it reevaluates fundamental questions such as "what is the definition of value?", "what does society look like when authority is decentralised?" In a context in which politics threatens to overwhelm our sense of justice and universalism, perhaps seeing the world through the lens of blockchain can help the cultural ecosystem find its feet.

I remember first telling Hans Ulrich about blockchain and Vitalik Buterin in early 2016, and I recall how he took an immediate interest in the concepts of decentralised technology. I knew that I had to put them together somehow, and combine these two worlds. Thus I invited Vitalik to meet Hans Ulrich. Though the two are professionally very distant, I feel that they are very close when it comes to the spirit of creation and critical thought. I hope that this will be the first of many conversations not only between Hans Ulrich and Vitalik, but between the people who make up the cultural and the blockchain communities.

—
Introduction by Jehan Chu
Interview by Hans Ulrich Obrist

Hello, Vitalik Buterin

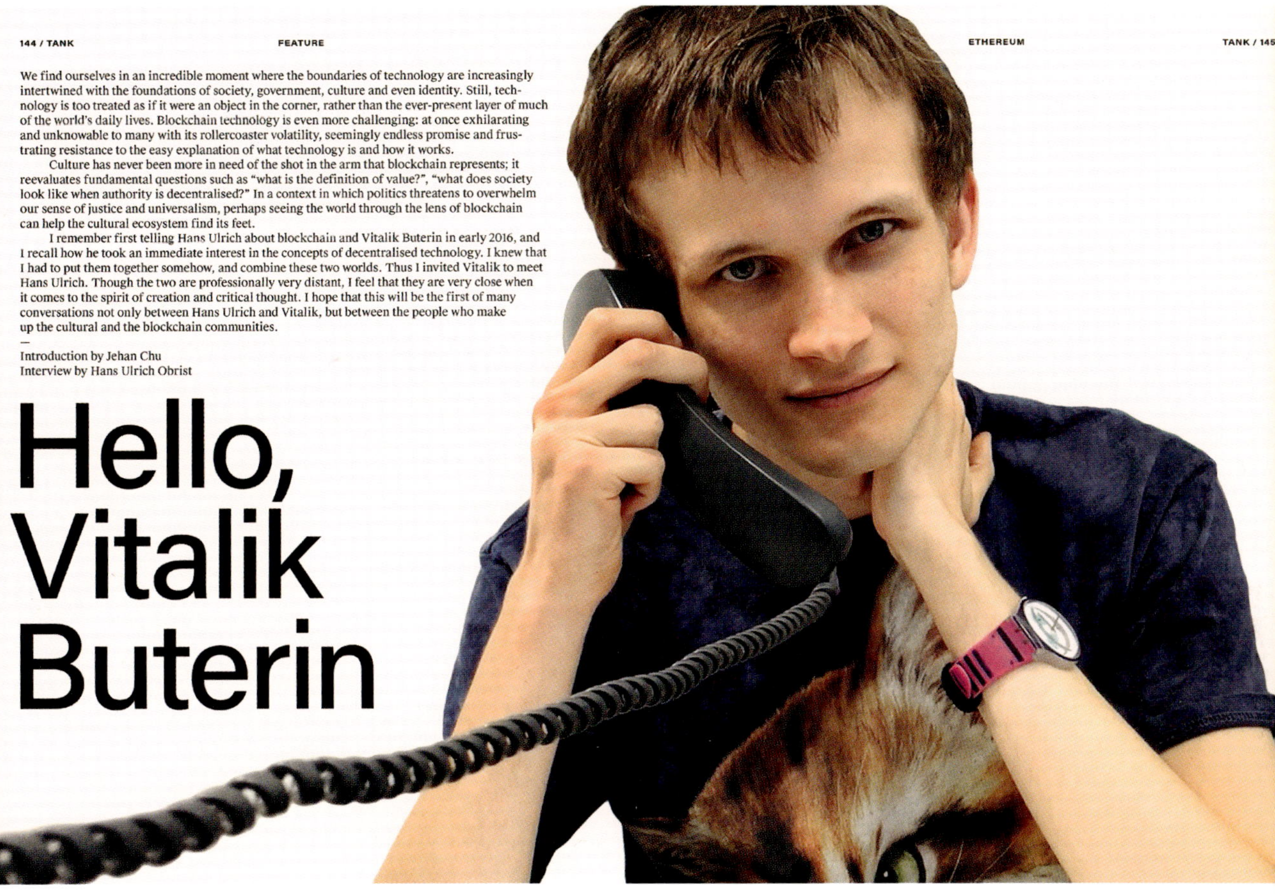

between the two of them was that he, Buterin, wanted to create a system that could conceive of himself as a villain. As David Yermack said, "I've told my colleagues that Vitalik is probably the most important person in finance, and the reactions that I get range from 'Who?' to 'You gotta be kidding me.' But I think his imagination to build out the Ethereum blockchain with all of the flexibility and versatility has been an immense contribution to this whole area."

This design for "the bad actor" is a hallmark of democracies. However unstable the U.S. democracy may currently be, it was originally designed to withstand having a bad person (a "bad man" in the language of that day) in office and for the system to survive. We might contrast that with other forms of governance—the autocrat who does whatever that person likes, or the philosopher king, the seemingly perfect person who can do no wrong and governs in the interest of all the people. The philosopher king requires people to agree on how they wish to be governed, and so the idea of designing a system in which oneself could be a villain is a radical act of democratic hopefulness and possibility.

Fig. 10
Vitalik Buterin,
still from *Tank
Magazine*, 2018.

2018
Christie's Art + Tech
Summit on blockchain

Buterin also designed Ethereum to be so easy to use that others would adopt it as a standard. In fact, when people mention NFTs, they are, again in the narrowest sense, referring to the ERC-721 non-fungible token on the Ethereum protocol. The analogy Buterin used was that "the stuff that came before Ethereum was a Swiss army knife. And Ethereum is like a Swiss army knife that contains a tiny built-in 3D printer that prints exactly what component you want to use on demand. . . ." Buterin continued, "Instead of defining the protocol in terms of things that you can do with it, define the protocol in terms of building blocks. And so, you can be kind of open-ended. A blockchain is this weird thing that's like somewhere right in between an open-source project, a corporation, and a country. I'd even add a fourth thing, which would be a language. Languages can be global. . . ."[14]

Buterin asked a key question: Why would you use blockchain when you could just use the Internet? His answer to this question became the governing principle of Ethereum and a guiding ethos in the democratic potential of blockchain: "The answer basically is that it's about trust." This is where it becomes crucial that he designed a trustless system—one in which he could be a villain. That capacity of blockchain sets up the democratic potential of the technology—for participation, for redistribution, and for a re-enlivening of the democratic experiment.

As mentioned in the introduction, when Beeple's *Everydays* was sold for 69 million dollars, it was bought by Vignesh Sundaresan—who goes by the moniker of MetaKovan—who immediately put the work into a fund called Metapurse and offered shares to the general public. You could have the "democratic" promise of owning a share in an artwork. What remains to be explored—in Chapter 4—is whether we are talking about participation in markets or about democracy itself.

THE ART STORY

NFTs are also at the center of an emergent creative practice that has grown substantially over the last decade. To recognize the story of NFTs as an art story is crucial to understanding what their impact on the art world might be. These digital tokens offer new modes of creating, of collecting, of curating, and of critiquing contemporary art. The way that NFTs are transacted, are consumed, and are displayed is beholden to a set of terms established over sixty years ago by artists who specifically aimed to create work that bypassed the market and decentralized production.

The impact of Sol LeWitt's wall drawings or the conceptual artist Fred Sandback's sculptures made of yarn (Fig. 11) was that the ideas defined the art and the ideas could be realized by anyone. Sandback created his works as sets of instructions regarding material and location of the yarn within the space of its installation. The magic of

Fig. 11
Fred Sandback, *Untitled*, 1976/1981. Venetian red acrylic yarn. Situational: spatial relationships established by the artist; overall dimensions vary with each installation.

● **2019**
Total sales of NFT art and collectibles estimated at $4.6 million

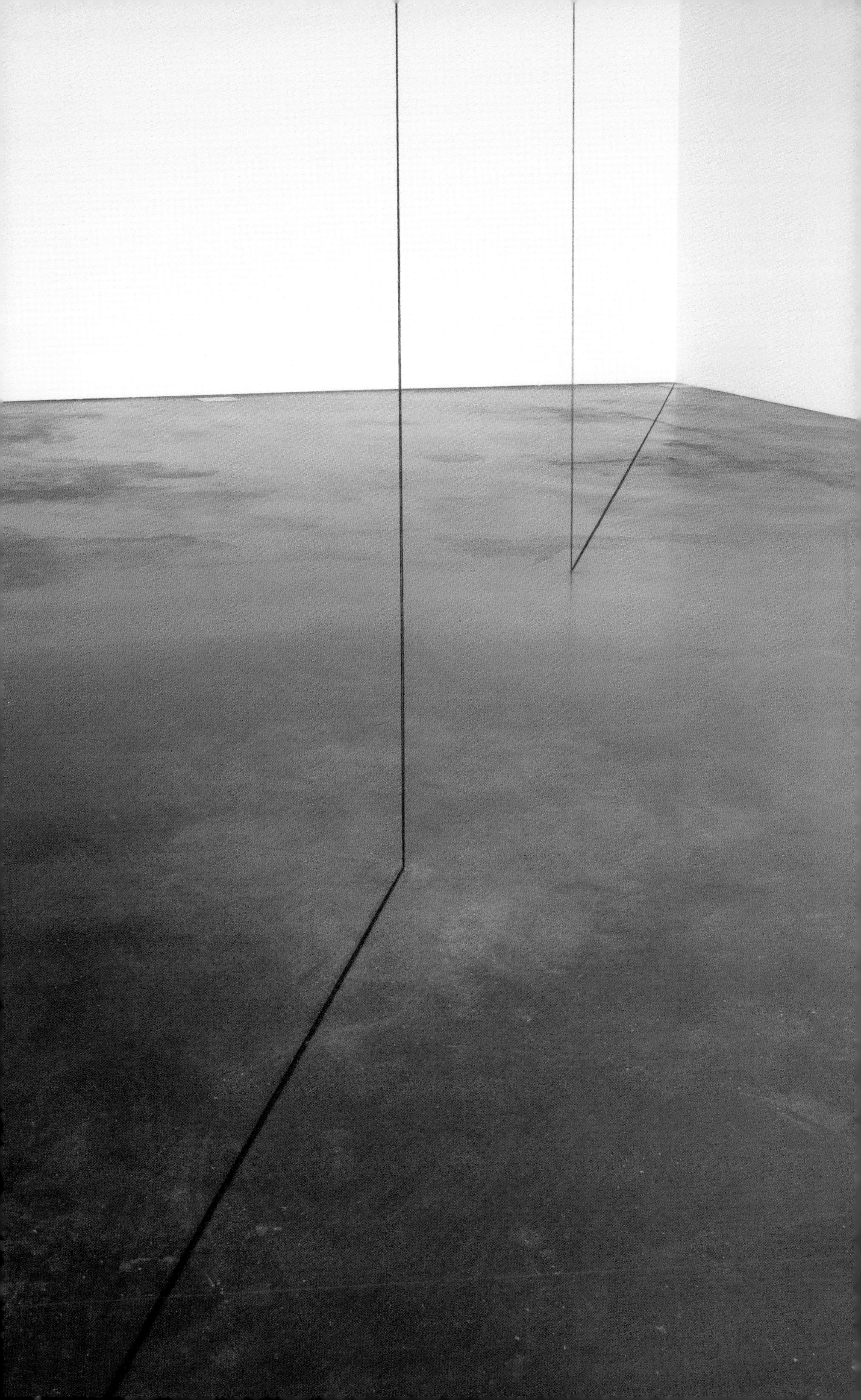

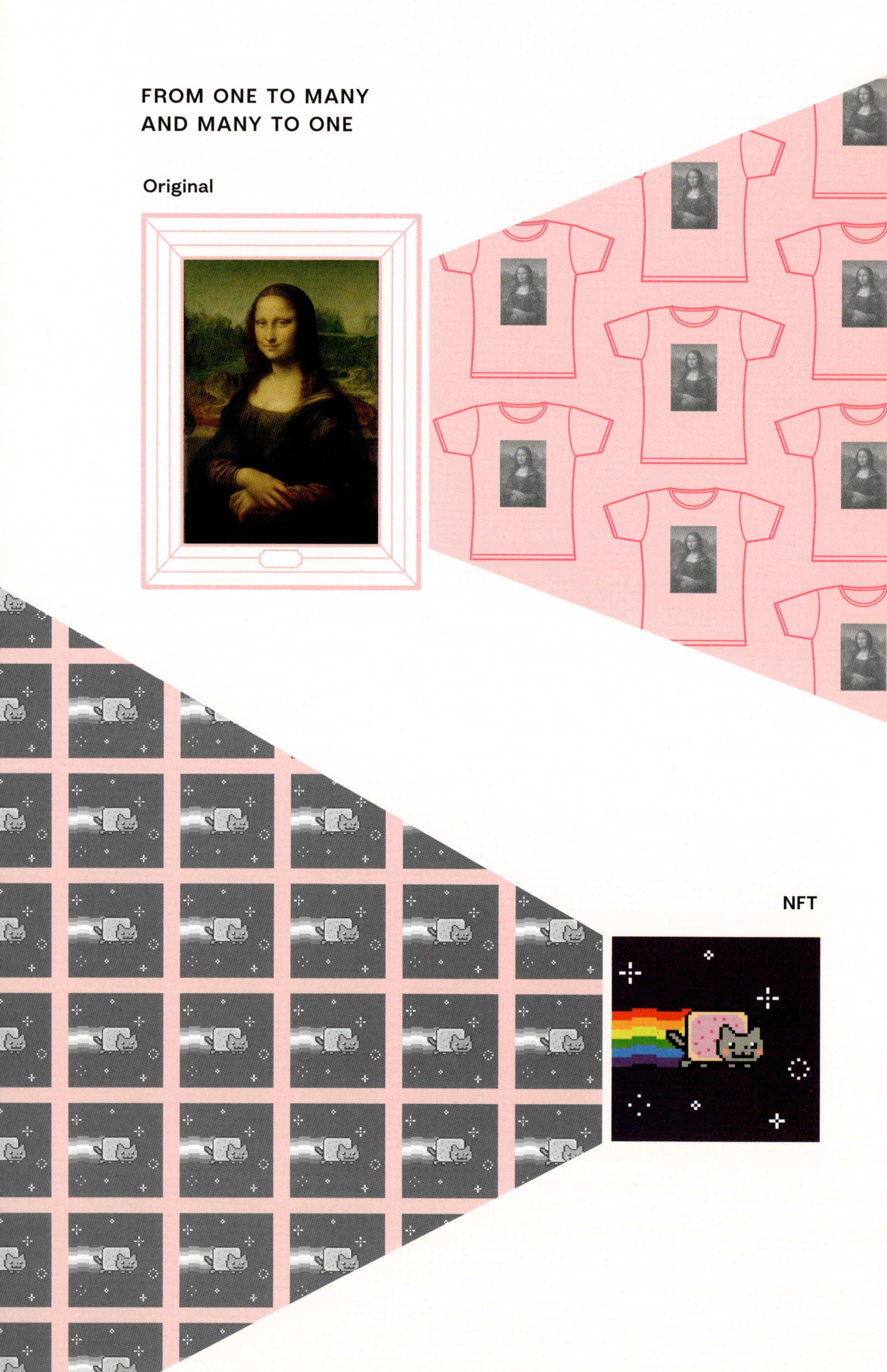
FROM ONE TO MANY
AND MANY TO ONE
Original
NFT

his practice was that his works are both site-specific and always in a state of changing, as the sites they inhabit are always shifting. Along with LeWitt and others, his creative approach also underscores how the origins of NFTs have an important artistic prologue. Collecting the work ultimately became about acquiring a document, a certificate of authenticity, that stated the instructions for production and indicated the owner of the work. For Sandback especially, the certificate provided a plan for materializing his minimal sculptures and also served as his signature that declared the work—the concept for the sculpture—to be his. As the artist noted in conversation in 2002,

> *a certificate accompanies [the sculptures] which gives the form of the piece, the material, and often some issue of the intention of how I have worked with it. It has a little stamp and a signature, which defines that thing after it has left my domain. So, the signature is on the certificate.*[15]

Decentralization on the one hand and clarity of authorship and ownership on the other remain foundational to the NFT story and braid together the dual ambitions of conceptual art and tokenization.

But tokenization also functions as a way to capture a single image out of a sea of copies. Art historians have engaged in debates regarding the originality of artworks for centuries, notably since mechanical reproduction afforded by the camera allowed for multiple copies of the same image to circulate at the same time. Rosalind Krauss deftly debunked the idea of valuing originality in her essay "Originality of the Avant-Garde and Other Modernist Myths," and in doing so made clear the challenges that modern technology brings to bear on how we process and value a copy versus an original. In this sense, NFTs move in the opposite direction: they single out an image and preserve it as an entity to be owned and valued distinctly differently from its digital brethren.

An artwork's originality bestows upon it a sense of primacy, singularity, and authority, which is what tokenization performs on digital images as it privileges one from many. The marketplace may take the specter of an original and reproduce it millions of times (for example, the *Mona Lisa* or another painting as reproduced on mugs, skateboards, socks, and stickers). The marketplace is also where the digital inversion of many copies to one original takes place (Fig. 12). NFTs move us from the marketplace of *Mona Lisa*–inspired merchandise to the singular digital image.

A digitally native example of this shift from one to many and then from many to one is that of the *Nyan Cat*. The *Nyan Cat* video had been circulating as a meme for a decade before it became an NFT in 2021, selling for 300 ether. As a digital asset, *Nyan Cat* illustrates how to make an original after the fact; but it's not the equivalent of an estate issuing a posthumous cast, which simply adds more copies to the

Fig. 12
From One to Many and Many to One.

2020
Change in deaccessioning policy at AAMD

marketplace. Instead, it establishes the authority and authenticity of the image and allows the existing copies to circulate freely. As a work of art, *Nyan Cat* is singular, but not unique; and as an NFT, it holds lessons for contemporary art about what we value when we have unlimited access to an image but significant restrictions as to how it can be used.

ARTIST STORIES

While art markets have typically focused on artworks—read: marquee prices—blockchain also opens new stories for artists. These stories concern serious power shifts in the arts ecosystem and new forms of economic sustainability that come from blockchain platforms' ability to provide artists with access to selling their work and also to receiving resale royalties, meaning payments that go back to artists when their work is resold. Artists have always faced—especially in contemporary times, post–patronage systems—a structural economic difficulty: they are asked to put work into the world before they know the value of it or before they are paid. Artists have engaged in creative activism—as early as Grant Wood, creator of *American Gothic,* in the United States and since the 1920s in France—to receive proceeds when their work resells.[16] In 1969, the Art Workers' Coalition lobbied for numerous powers to go to artists. An enduring legacy of that work is the Artist's Contract, a model document written by gallerist Seth Siegelaub and attorney Robert Projansky. The contract has many terms, including artists' control over future exhibition and the right to know who owns their work.[17] However, the most famous term is a resale royalty, granting the artist 15 percent when their work changes hands. Such royalties—*droit de suite* in France and artist resale right in the United Kingdom—exist in over seventy jurisdictions worldwide, but not in the United States. Blockchain has taken what was a somewhat conceptual economic experiment and given it legs, in the form of dramatically reduced transaction costs to administer. For instance, the platform SuperRare pays a 10 percent resale royalty, and many other platforms have followed suit. Thus, artists can make more money both by selling their works directly—sometimes circumventing the galleries that would otherwise take 50 percent—and by receiving proceeds in the secondary market.

The artist story of NFTs is also a new version of the perennial problem of labor. Does a work of art take five minutes or a lifetime of training? The Beeple work is a study of labor in the sense that the creator made a work every day for thirteen years. (However, as Ben Davis noted, the auction price translates to 14,000 dollars per day, again distinguishing the work by its price and not its content.) But to look at any artwork through the lens of labor is to consider the inherently awkward overlap of art and economics. Arguably, this is the most interesting part of the project.

2021
Beeple's *Everydays* sells at
Christie's for $69.346 million

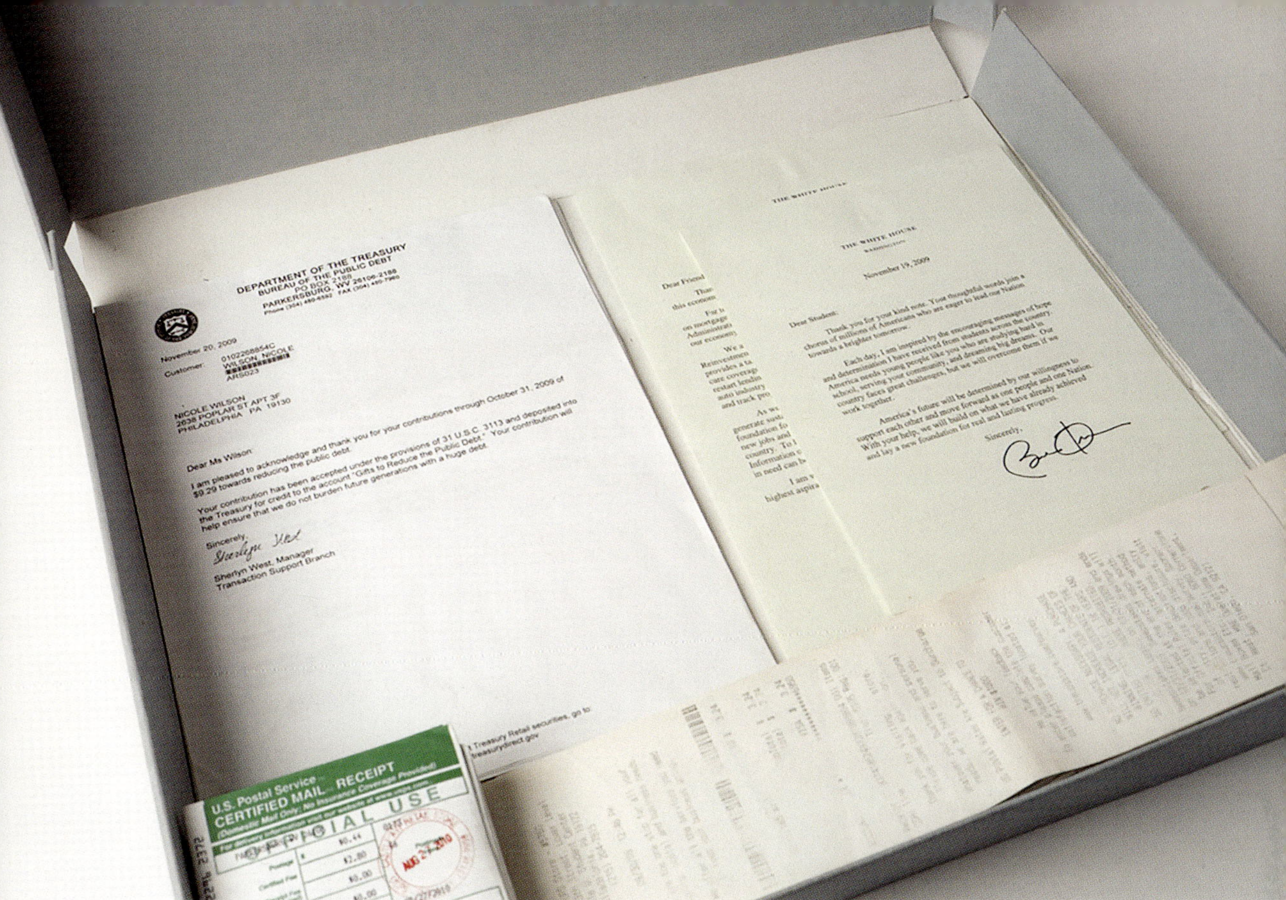

If labor is a compelling part of the Beeple story, then it begs the question, why not value other projects in labor? Why that one? On August 31, 2009—within a year after the Satoshi paper and the LeWitt retrospective at MASS MoCA—the artist Nicole Wilson started another artwork of labor and constancy: the *National Debt Project* (Fig. 13). Spooked, as many of her generation were, by the looming national debt, months into post-financial-crisis monetary policy and bank bailouts, Wilson began to collect spare change she saw on the sidewalk and to send it to the federal government to, in her way and as a conceptual project, alleviate the national debt. She kept careful records. Every day, she would mail the change she found to the Bureau of the Public Debt (later named the Bureau of the Fiscal Service), under the auspices of the U.S. Treasury Department. She sent the change via certified mail with a copy to the White House. (On days she found no change, she mailed in one penny of her own.) From August 31, 2009, to May 10, 2022, she sent in $534.32 at a cost to her of $20,016.21.[18]

Fig. 13
Nicole Wilson, *National Debt Project*, August 2009–ongoing. Mixed media performance using paper, US coins, certified mail, and digital project archive.

CONCLUSION

It is hard to know which artists will ascend through markets, whose work will be fashionable in their time and then stored in museum basements, whose work will have staying power, and who will prove to be ahead of their time in ways that are conceptually brain-breaking. Haber and Stornetta seem to have been such artists ahead of their time, while conceptual art pioneers LeWitt and Sandback advanced a type of practice in the 1960s and 1970s that circumvented the market, only to be consumed by it in subsequent decades. LeWitt's critiques of commerce, by drawing directly on the wall and then using certificates of authenticity, both echoes and converges with Haber and Stornetta's obsessions with knowledge in a digital age. And now both projects have been simultaneously subsumed by and influential on the markets—general or art markets—in which they operate.

The knowledge story that launched Haber and Stornetta's work is the basis of provenance, or history of ownership, that is a key contribution of blockchain within the arts and outside. David Yermack, the New York University finance professor and blockchain expert, summed it up: "Provenance is almost a timeless problem.... The importance of the blockchain is really to establish provenance.... What the blockchain gives us is a way to keep track of these things with unconditional certainty." This resonates strikingly with what LeWitt expert Chris Vacchio shared about the artist's approach to finding a solution for declaring ownership of his work—his ideas, his knowledge. As Vacchio said,

> *At the very beginning, [LeWitt] didn't have a really strong idea of how he wanted to sell [the wall drawings] and how he wanted ownership of essentially [his] ideas to work. He would write in all caps, "this is a certificate," but it wasn't until the mid-1980s when he had his first print catalogue raisonné, which is an accounting of all his wall drawings up until that point, that he decided to go back and standardize and have an official printed and signed certificate for every single wall drawing. [And] those are the certificates that are still used today.*[19]

The capacity of blockchain to register these certificates—and many other forms of ownership and provenance—has vast influence beyond the arts as well. "What I tell my students in finance classes is this is an innovation on par with double entry bookkeeping," Yermack said, "which came in seven hundred years ago in the Renaissance. . . . It's the biggest thing in financial accounting in seven hundred–odd years, but it's also something that maps very easily into supply chain, into medical records, government records, border security. And, of course, the arts." That authentication could apply to any industry, to supply chains for everything from baby food to pharmaceuticals to luxury goods to financial transactions. The applications also called anyone's bluff on what it might mean to engage politically in markets. Yermack was invoking market tools to address the environmental problem, and warning a generation of financiers that their career trajectories were being upended. Kevin McCoy, the artist who made the first NFT in 2014, said that when he first started to learn about the technology obsessively in the Bitcoin

2021
Total sales of NFT art and
collectibles estimated at $11.1 billion

Talk chatroom, "Politically, it was one of those things where it's so fringy that you can't actually figure out if it's really, really left-wing or really, really right-wing."[20]

Contemplating the span of art history from the Renaissance to the present, and the changes in patronage, artistic working style, and power, is blockchain the biggest artistic intervention since the Renaissance? What seismic shifts will it bring in the power structure of the arts? Many other questions will still need to be answered—from the environmental impact to the possibility of regulation that is at all workably designed.

It is possible art will be subsumed into the larger development of blockchain and NFTs in popular culture—and equally possible that art will offer up answers of consequence to those larger fields. What is at stake and what we explore in the rest of this book are the questions of truth, money, politics, economics, markets, and art—sources of meaning, as ways we organize how we live together, and as ways forward in the creative re-imagination of our democracy.

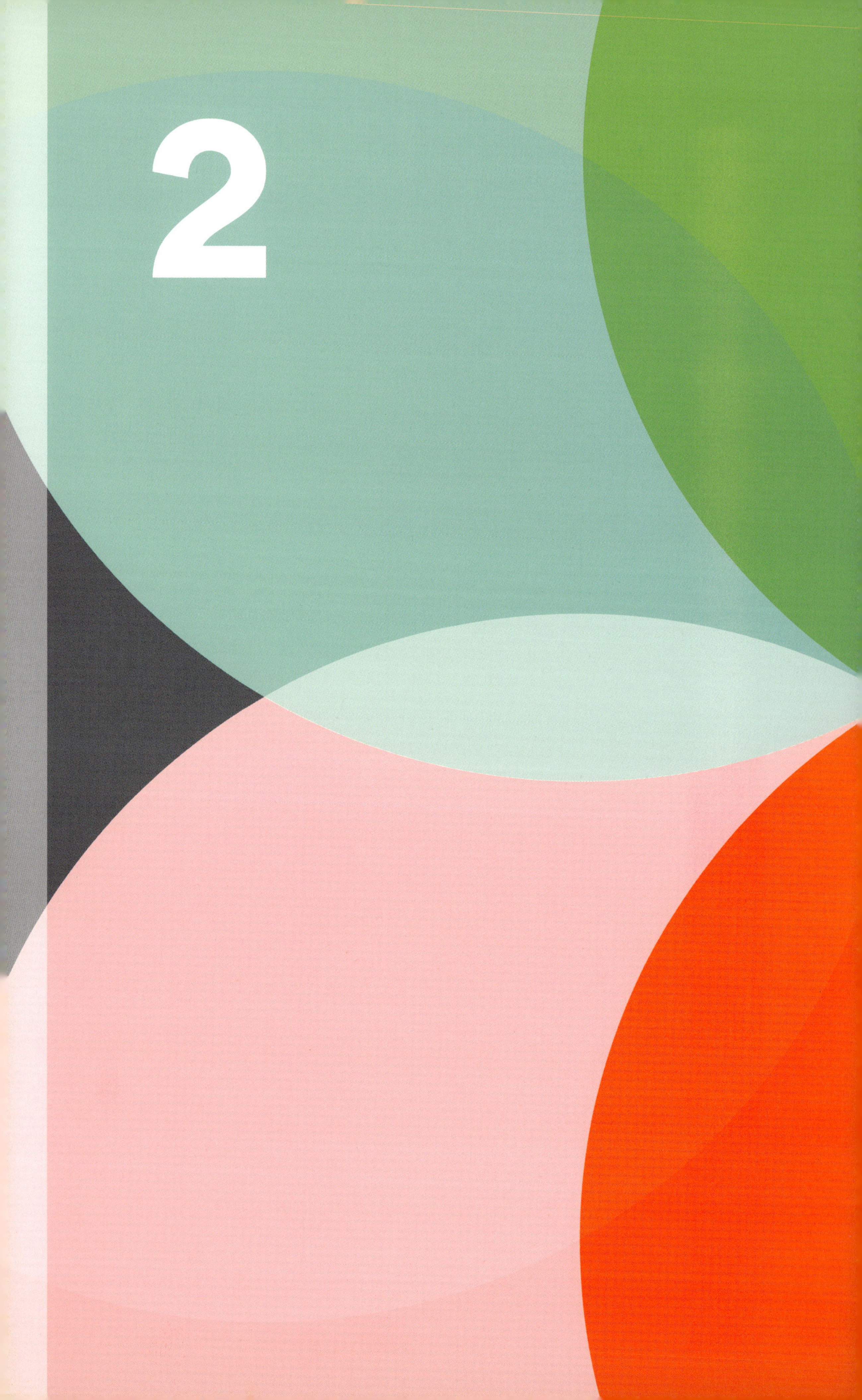

2

ARTISTS
+ MAKING

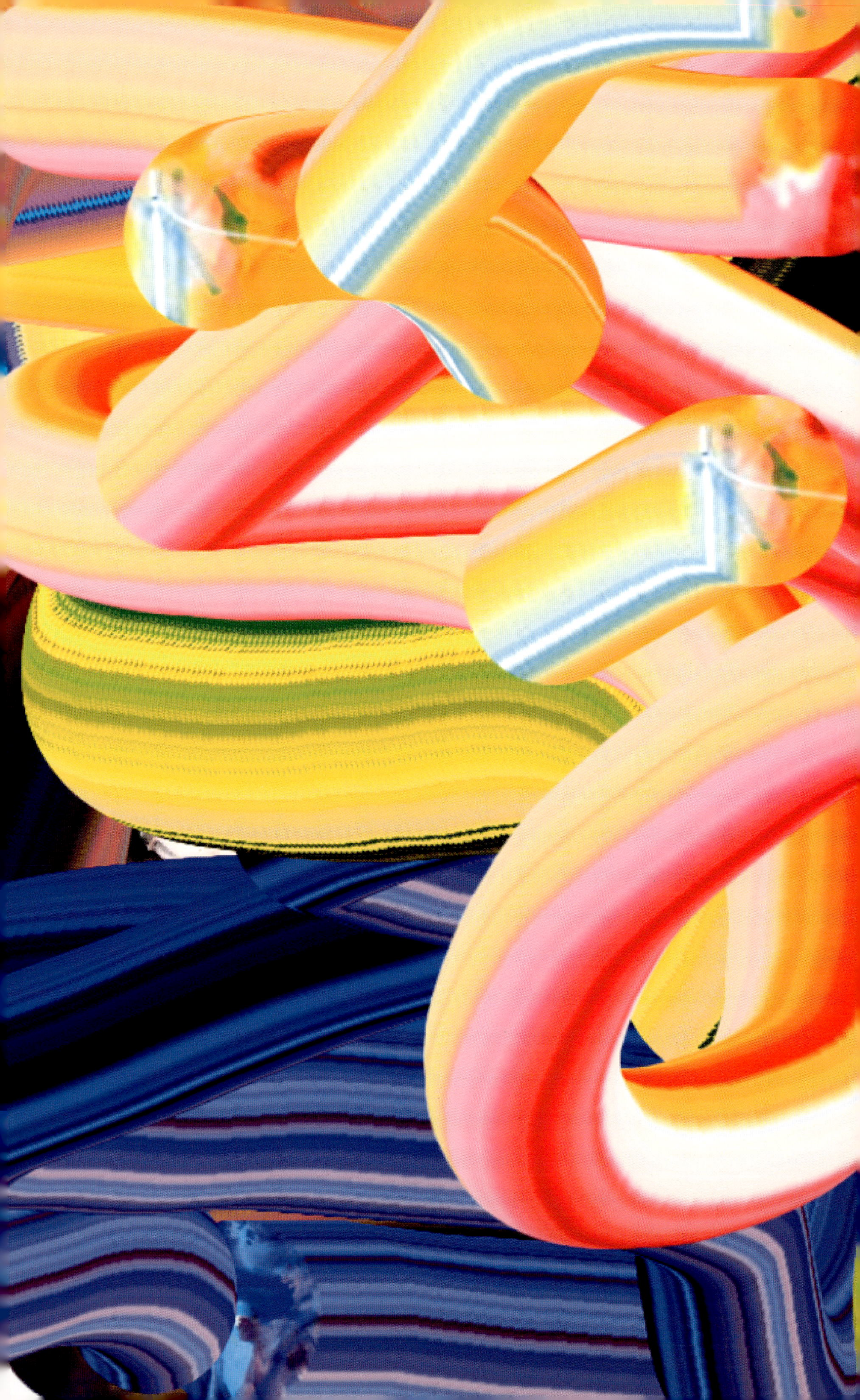

*I think the reason I am in the role that I am in and the
reason that I've chosen the career that I have is because
I think artists are always the seers or the truth tellers.
They show us the way forward.*

—NORA BURNETT ABRAMS

ON APRIL 11, 1980, AT 7:00 P.M., the artist Tehching Hsieh commenced a performance by punching a time clock. According to the statement he wrote, the performance would end one year later, on April 11, 1981, at 6:00 p.m. During that year, he would punch into the clock every hour—not every hour of a workday, but every hour of an entire day. Hsieh developed a system to ensure—transparently—that he had adhered to his own rules. This "Explanation of Procedure for Sam Hsieh's One Year Performance" included several stipulations. First, he would have a witness sign each day's timecard for a total of 366 cards. Second, the witness would "sign and seal" the time clock itself and return to be present in the event any repairs became necessary. Third, Hsieh would document the project on film. Hsieh wrote, "With a 16mm movie camera, I shall document each time I punch the Time Clock by shooting one frame. At the completion

Fig. 1
Addie
Wagenknecht,
*Rainbow
Eugene Man*
(detail), 2021.
Digital work
utilizing sext
and "dick pics"
received in
Instagram DMs
from 2015 to
2018 in a body
of paintings
using custom
computational
brushes.

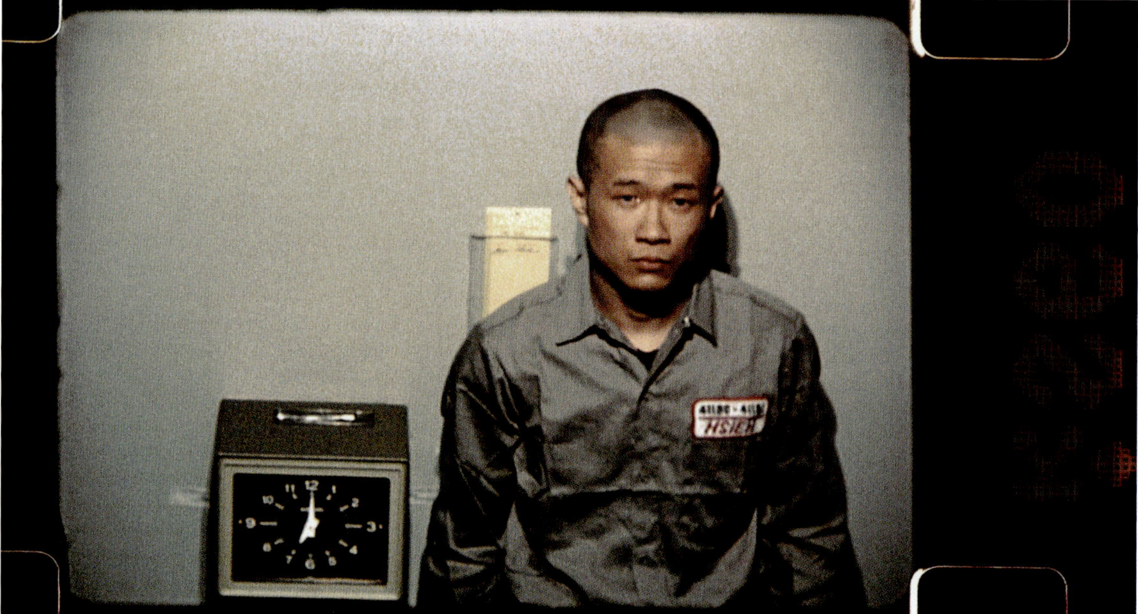

of the performance, the witness will confirm that the film is unedited." Lastly, Hsieh decided to give the performance another temporal marker by shaving his head at the outset and allowing his hair to grow back over the course of the year.[21]

A few different observations spring from this project, both in and of itself and in relation to this journey into NFTs. First, Hsieh embodies the dignity of artistic commitment, the show and not tell of the giving of self to the work of art. He created a chart documenting when he missed punching in. Out of the 8,760 possible punch-ins, he missed 134, or 1.54 percent. Only 93 of these misses were for sleeping, which, considering the 24-hour nature of the project, seems rather superhuman. The only other times he failed to punch in were related to punching in early (10 times) or late (31 times).

The "witness" to the project was David Milne, at the time the executive director of the Foundation for the Community of Artists in New York City. Milne essentially served an audit function, but in the more humane-sounding form of bearing witness. Other projects subsequently—Marina Abramović's *The Artist Is Present* perhaps being the most famous—have asked artists to involve their bodies in their work by way of durational projects. Abramovic's work was witnessed by the crowd. One could have theoretically stood at the Museum of Modern Art or in other venues and watched the artist sit in a chair for seven hours at a stretch, six days each week.[22] Hsieh's work was more private and more extreme, taking over the entirety of his life, one hour at a time. We trusted Milne as the central authority, and, of course, we had no reason not to, and no reason in particular to wish to

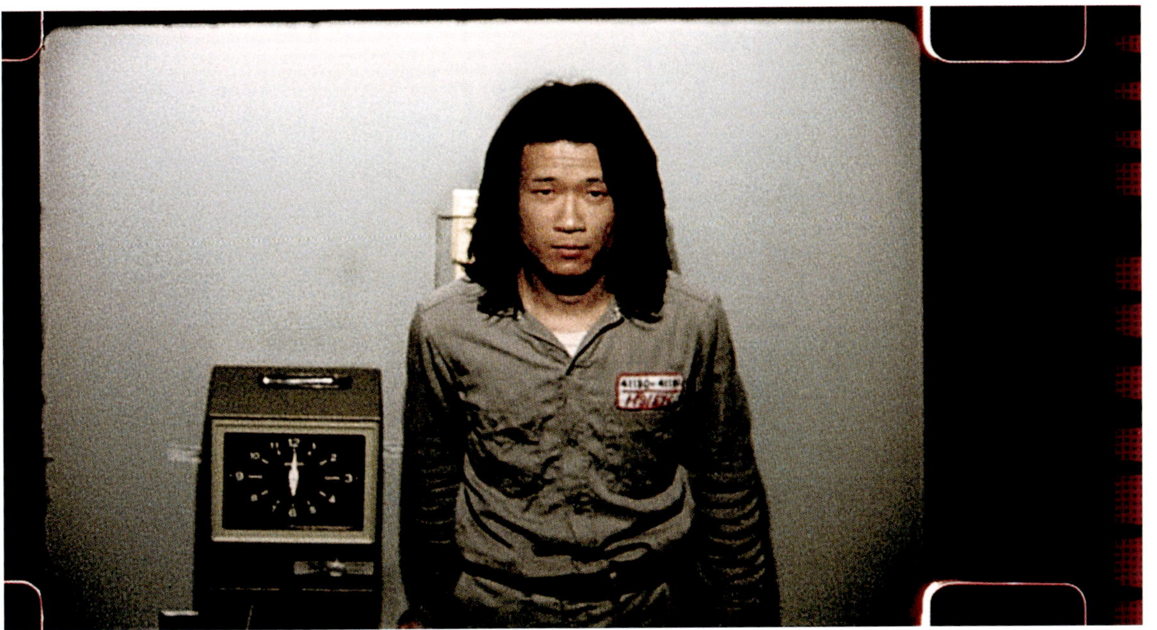

replace him with a mechanical system. That said, Hsieh's work is instructive in thinking about the building of blockchain as what *The Economist* magazine called a "trust machine" and in the form of registration of artworks by asking others—lone authorities or the whole world—to bear witness.

Hsieh's work quietly surpasses by orders of magnitude the labor study of Beeple's *Everydays.* Labor can be a necessity of art, an input that sometimes has no causal bearing on the output, and a conceptual subject that becomes especially important when we consider how NFTs change the world for artists and making. Recall that LeWitt didn't know how to price his first wall drawing and so he charged for the time it took to make it. Yet, Hsieh's work would be unlikely to be understood in this way—not as labor but as commitment, not as conversant and commensurate with market but as human. The separation of art and labor is also part of what gives art its specialness—what Lewis Hyde calls "the gift," or the essence of the work that is not commodifiable or reducible to a market, even if the work can be bought and sold.[23] Recent examples of artists for whom labor, duration, and discipline become their mediums abound. Lenka Clayton's drawings are made only using keys found on a 1957 Smith-Corona Skyriter typewriter and Tim Youd's project *100 Novels* is a multi-year performance in which the artist retypes a seminal work of fiction within a gallery space that connects geographically or thematically with the central ideas of the book. To date, he has retyped 66 novels in spaces across the United States and Europe.

These ideas of labor are important to the NFT story for artists, because artists are asked to engage in labor before they are paid.

Fig. 3
Tehching Hsieh,
*One Year
Performance
1980–1981 Last
Hour.* Still.

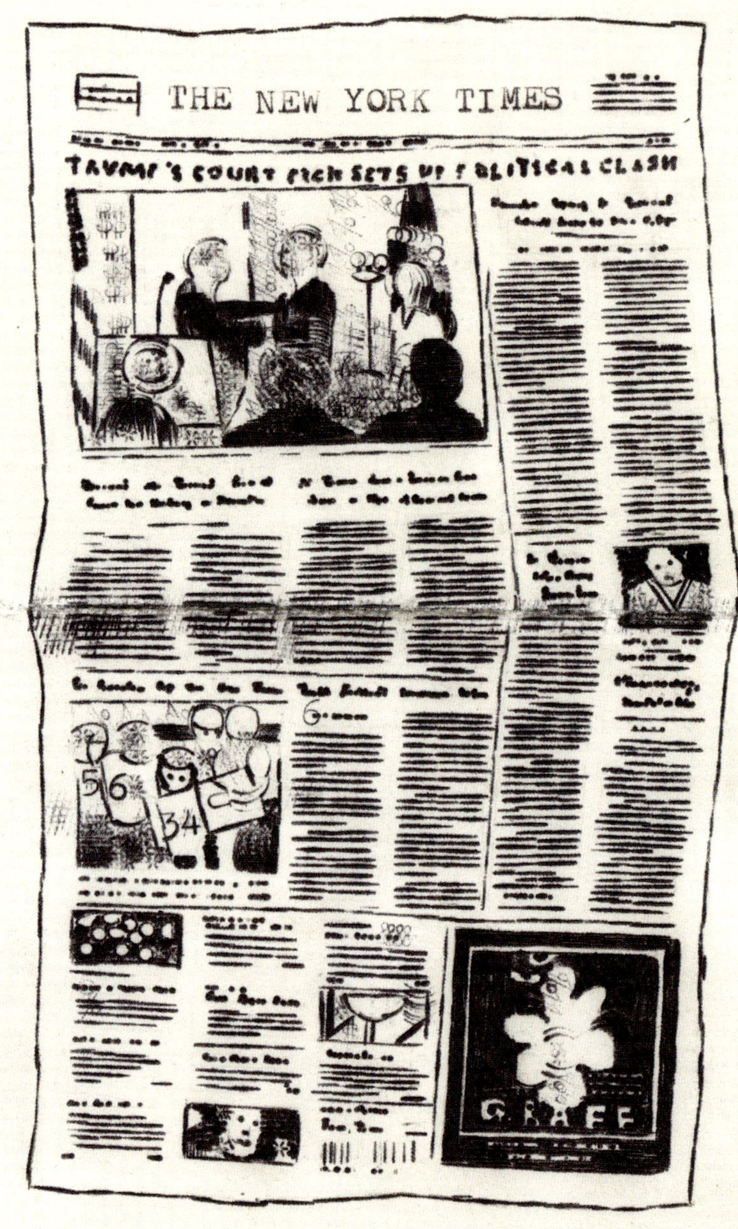

1st FEBRUARY 2017

They are often making work on spec, without commission or artist's fee, taking on all the costs and fronting the contingency and general risk that their work may not sell and that they will be paid—traditionally 50 percent of the gallery sales price—after the work is sold. Thus, the artist story of NFTs is braided with new avenues of economic sustainability, expansive explorations of digital art—with digital scarcity now possible. Artists are also probing NFTs as part of an institutional critique of art markets and engagement with, as in the work of Dread Scott, the idea of fungibility as inseparable—vis-à-vis culpability—from the slave trade.

The labor of making art has a history of being simply strange. Pablo Picasso famously made a five-minute drawing on a napkin and then explained it had taken him decades, actually, to be able to do that. Artistic labor is no less peculiar for NFTs.

We begin with the first art NFT in the story of Kevin McCoy, his longtime collaborator, Jennifer McCoy, and his technology partner in the first NFT, Anil Dash. Kevin McCoy is widely credited with making the first NFT, *Quantum*, in 2014, and did so in a very short period of time. He also made the work in an incidental way, in order to show Anil Dash, the technologist with whom he had been paired for the New Museum and Rhizome's sixth edition of its Seven on Seven program, how to register something to a blockchain. But McCoy could easily make the Picasso argument about how that NFT sat in his larger body of work—and how novelty, effort, and value interact not just for art markets but for artists, and more specifically for the dignity and difficulties of artistic labor.

McCoy more commonly collaborates with his wife, Jennifer McCoy. The two met in Paris shortly after college. Kevin had nearly sought a Ph.D. in philosophy and then, in his collaborations with Jennifer, found philosophy within artistic practice or, as Kevin said, went from being a reader to a maker. Some of their early work seems particularly laborious—and glorious: They once put Raymond Bellour's system of film analysis into practice by building a classification system for the television show *Starsky & Hutch*. They watched twenty episodes of the first season, broke them down shot by shot, and made a database of 278 categories—every girlfriend, apartment building, scene with ominous music, and so on.[24]

Fig. 4
Lenka Clayton, *1st February 2017*, 2017, from *Typewriter Drawings.* Ink on paper, made with 1957 Smith-Corona Skyriter typewriter.

They have worked jointly on blockchain, including a 2019 piece collected by the Whitney Museum of American Art in which fifty members of the public could apply to be donors of record of a 16mm film, *Public Key/Private Key*, that itself contained an alphanumeric code associated with blockchain.[25] As Jennifer tells the story, Kevin's interest in blockchain came about around 2012 and then took hold more obsessively in 2013, when he started to mysteriously disappear from the dinner table after their family meal. Jennifer described it:

57

Slowly I realized that he was just spending more and more time on the computer, and without really saying much about what was going on. And then, slowly, he kind of revealed that there was this thing called the blockchain and it seemed kind of interesting. And, as a philosophy person, he's always interested in systems and different systems and, and this one was about currency, which I thought was super boring. But then he'd have these little rendezvous in Brooklyn when I'd be like, "You're going to buy Bitcoin at like ten o'clock at night on the corner? Bring the dog." You know, like where . . . who is this shady thing?

It was the early days of Bitcoin, as Jennifer said—on the one hand "very much like Silk Road drug transactions" and on the other hand "some pretty utopian interesting ideas about decentralization and community building, a kind of a bottom-up structure." And it was a universe unto itself—what Kevin called a "terrarium world." In the same way that Kevin and Jennifer had tried to deconstruct and classify things, Jennifer watched Kevin start to do the same for Bitcoin and blockchain. At first the work seemed most likely to help their fellow digital artist friends. Digital art was hard to sell—meaning it was hard to sustain a creative practice on—because of the lack of digital scarcity. Blockchain could allow digital works to have unique identifiers and, in Jennifer's recollection, that seemed an application that could help their friends.

Kevin's expertise started to become known within their community of artists and friends. Jennifer had a T-shirt made that Kevin frequently wore, which read, "Ask me about blockchain technology," because when they were out, she said, she would eventually "find Kevin in a corner surrounded by six confused people as he again broke down, what is blockchain?" The use cases of provenance—having an essentially irrefutable history of ownership of an object—or digital scarcity—being able to survive better as a digital-first artist—were becoming understood (at least in the party groupings around Kevin) but would not enter the mainstream, even the edge of the fray of the mainstream, for several years, or as Jennifer put it, after "a zillion magazine articles and some auction results."

Some of those magazine articles covered *Quantum*. The Seven on Seven collaboration created the crucible in which Kevin's years of thinking about blockchain and taking the dog (Roy) to late-night Brooklyn Bitcoin meet-ups could come to fruition—the decades of practice that leads to the short span of creating the work itself. Kevin said of working with Anil Dash, "When we met, I'm like, 'We're going to make a blockchain provenance thing.' And he's like, 'Okay, that sounds cool.' It was all built in twenty-four hours."

Dash and McCoy were working in the offices of Wieden+Kennedy, an advertising agency that had provided space for the event. McCoy and Dash sat in a glassed-in conference room "with a bar in it … You know, all the snacks and great architecture—the full-on kind of thing," McCoy said. Against that backdrop, Dash asked McCoy what they were going to do. McCoy said, "'I'm going to show you how we're going to do this.' And I manually went through the steps, like, 'Here's the artwork.' I had this animated GIF that made it look really cool." McCoy explained the metadata and more technical aspects, and then once he had uploaded the work to his website, they posted a Tweet to launch the work. The Tweet went into the metadata of the work's blockchain listing on Namecoin, and that became the first art NFT. Kevin said the work intentionally was a flash of light, or the beginning of something. The second NFT, which is the one they used in the Seven on Seven demo, came from looped footage Jennifer had made of a parking lot viewed from a high floor when the McCoys were at NYU Abu Dhabi.

Kevin McCoy joked, "The whole thing was done in a couple of hours." The remainder of their time was spent thinking of names for the platform on which the NFT was registered; eventually they landed on Monegraph for monetized graphic, a nod to the singularity implied in the more common art-world usage of "monograph" to describe a book either on one artist or by one author. Although *Quantum* was made on the Namecoin blockchain, Dash and McCoy would go on to found a company by the name of Monegraph that registered artists' work on the Bitcoin blockchain and then later the Ethereum blockchain and that paid artists resale royalties and allowed them to set licensing terms for their work.

Quantuum predates the NFT technically, but "NFT" is used broadly to describe a unique, blockchain-identified record, often connected to some sort of object, such as an image or film clip. Technically, an NFT is an ERC-721 non-fungible token on the Ethereum blockchain. (As described in Chapter 1, "ERC" stands for "Ethereum Request for Comments" and is the way that proposals for new programming standards are named.) Because *Quantum* predates Ethereum, it was later moved from Namecoin and reminted on Ethereum. *Quantum* sold in the Natively Digital Sotheby's sale in the summer of 2021 for 1.47 million dollars.[26]

McCoy said:

All these developments at the technical level were [also] happening at the discursive and discussion level. [People] were building the system from scratch; they were not bogged down by the problems of the art market. And so, in these Ethereum marketplaces that started coming on in 2017, they just built splits in and that became a norm. It became more of a social norm that now has carried on and it is hard to imagine that it would get dislodged. [With] the dollar amounts involved, the art world has to respond [and] take notice. And so, some of those effects are gonna trickle back to the physical world.[27]

While the sale of *Quantum* may seem a money story—even a cynical one—we can share, with permission, that while we were filming the McCoys for the MCA Denver series, Kevin was sorting out some of the complexity of *Quantum* having been moved from Namecoin to Ethereum. Kevin retained the private key to the name, meaning he could prove his ownership of it within the cryptographic systems of blockchain. But the move was later litigated because an Internet actor who may or may not have earned the moniker "troll" made a version of the Namecoin registration with a different private key. The Sotheby's sale surely made the McCoys look like deep-pocketed targets. In fact, true to Kevin's own origin story as a reader who became a maker, he used the proceeds from the sale of *Quantum* to save for his children's college education and to buy himself two books. One of the books, acquired with a 50 percent discount, was *The Collected Works of Samuel Taylor Coleridge, Volume 8: Lectures 1818–1819: On the History of Philosophy*.

TIMELINE OF BLOCKCHAIN

We place *Quantum* as the first art NFT on a timeline (as appears on the facing page and across the footer of the prior chapters), before delving more into both digital artistic practice beyond NFTs and NFT engagement as conceptual practice.[28]

60

ADDIE WAGENKNECHT

There are many motivations behind artists' engagement with blockchain technology and minting NFTs, but Addie Wagenknecht's interest fluidly moves between the more traditional spaces of conceptual artistic production and those of the digital realm. "I would explain my artistic practice as primarily research and study–based works, where I tend to use visual language or tools to explain or express things that I find I can't do in any other medium, be it words or speaking, math or computer science."

Her practice remains distinct for how she has investigated blockchain as part of her research and also worked within blockchain-based companies. As a technology professional and an artist, she has scrutinized, experimented with, and furthered the capabilities of this technology. She is a digital artist who also works as a programmer for the layer one protocols, meaning for blockchain structures (e.g., Ethereum, Bitcoin, and newer blockchains such as Tezos and Algorand) themselves. Wagenknecht has advised the executive teams for different platforms, as well as minting her own NFTs.

Wagenknecht began exploring blockchain in its early days, having been introduced to it through her involvement with open-source communities and the appeal

DEVELOPMENT OF BLOCKCHAIN

1968 Sol LeWitt's first wall drawing at Paula Cooper Gallery

1983 Apple IIe computer released

1989 15% of U.S. households have a computer

1991 Stuart Haber and Scott Stornetta publish "How to Time-Stamp a Digital Document" in the *Journal of Cryptology*

1998 Founding of Google

2000 U.S. Supreme Court decides *Bush v. Gore,* making George W. Bush U.S. president

2004 Founding of Facebook

2006 Founding of Twitter

2007 Reality show *Keeping Up with the Kardashians* debuts

2008 Fall of Lehman Brothers and start of global financial crisis

LeWitt retrospective launches at MASS MoCA

Satoshi Nakamoto circulates Bitcoin white paper, building a currency around Haber and Stornetta's time-stamping

2009 Satoshi Nakamoto launches Bitcoin blockchain

2010 U.S. Supreme Court decides *Citizens United v. Federal Election Commission*

Bitcoin Pizza Day

2012 Meni Rosenfeld proposes colored coins, a precursor to NFTs

2014 Kevin McCoy makes first NFT

DADA launches

2015 Vitalik Buterin launches Ethereum blockchain

2017 Larva Labs (Matt Hall and John Watkinson) launch *CryptoPunks*

Dapper Labs launches CryptoKitties

2018 ERC-721 formalized by Ethereum consortium

Christie's Art + Tech Summit on blockchain

2019 Total sales of NFT art and collectibles estimated at $4.6 million

2020 Change in deaccessioning policy at AAMD

2021 Beeple's *Everydays* sells at Christie's for $69.346 million

2021 Total sales of NFT art and collectibles estimated at $11.1 billion

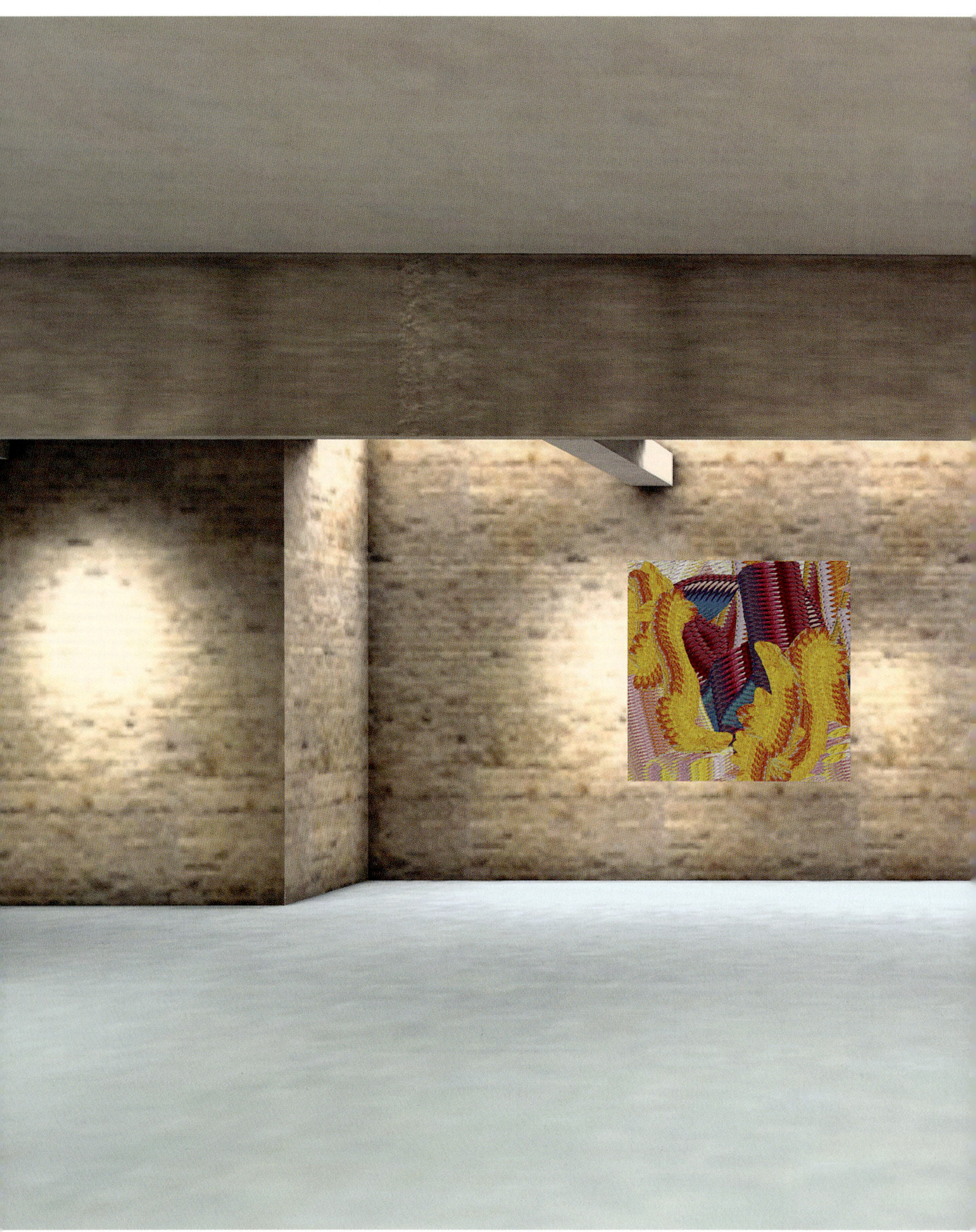

Fig. 5
Addie
Wagenknecht,
*Thinking of
You*, 2021.
Installation view,
KÖNIG DIGITAL,
Decentraland,
2021.

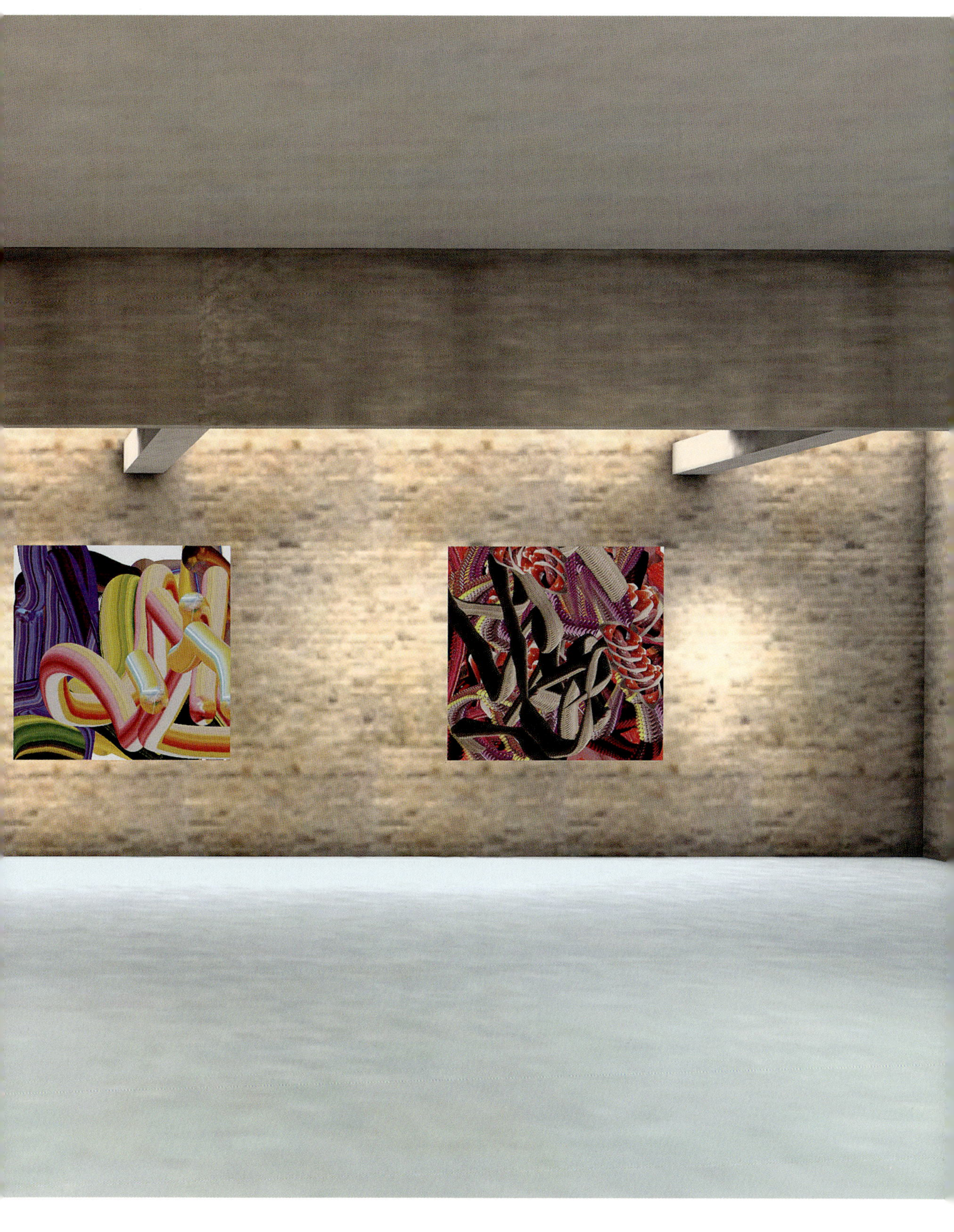

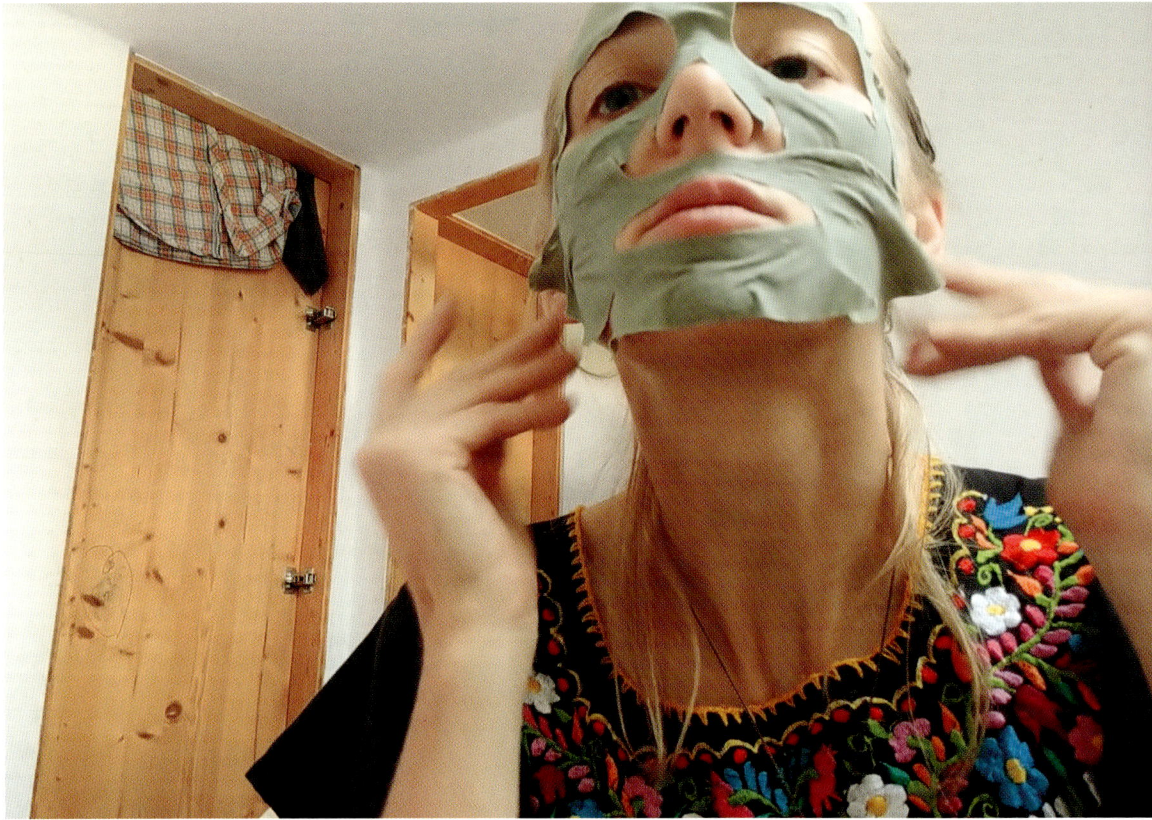

of a digital "creative commons." What distinguishes her engagement with block-chain is that she straddles both the innovative side of the technology's development and deployment and the traditional art world with gallery representation, artistic commissions, and museum projects. Her ability to move seamlessly between two seemingly disparate realms made the technology more accommodating of creative practice, and her creative practice has made her an active participant in navigating the "hyperspace gold rush" of the 2020s. "Everyone was just knocking at my door because they had this faint idea that I had been working with NFTs prior to that. So, now it's sort of a parallel track in my artistic practice, primarily as an advisor, but also as a user."

Creatively, the intersection between her research-based practice and her technical expertise has generated remarkable projects, both as physical installations in traditional spaces and as exhibitions in the metaverse, an alternative, digital environment replete with purposeful spaces, identities, and cultural and social practices. In 2021, Wagenknecht participated in König Galerie's exhibition *The Artist Is Online,* which took place in Decentraland, which was first developed in 2015 and then launched in 2017 as one of the original

Fig. 6
Addie Wagenknecht, *Korean Sheet Masks and Password Management for Pore-Refining Wins*, 2018, from *Self Care and Crypto*. Still.

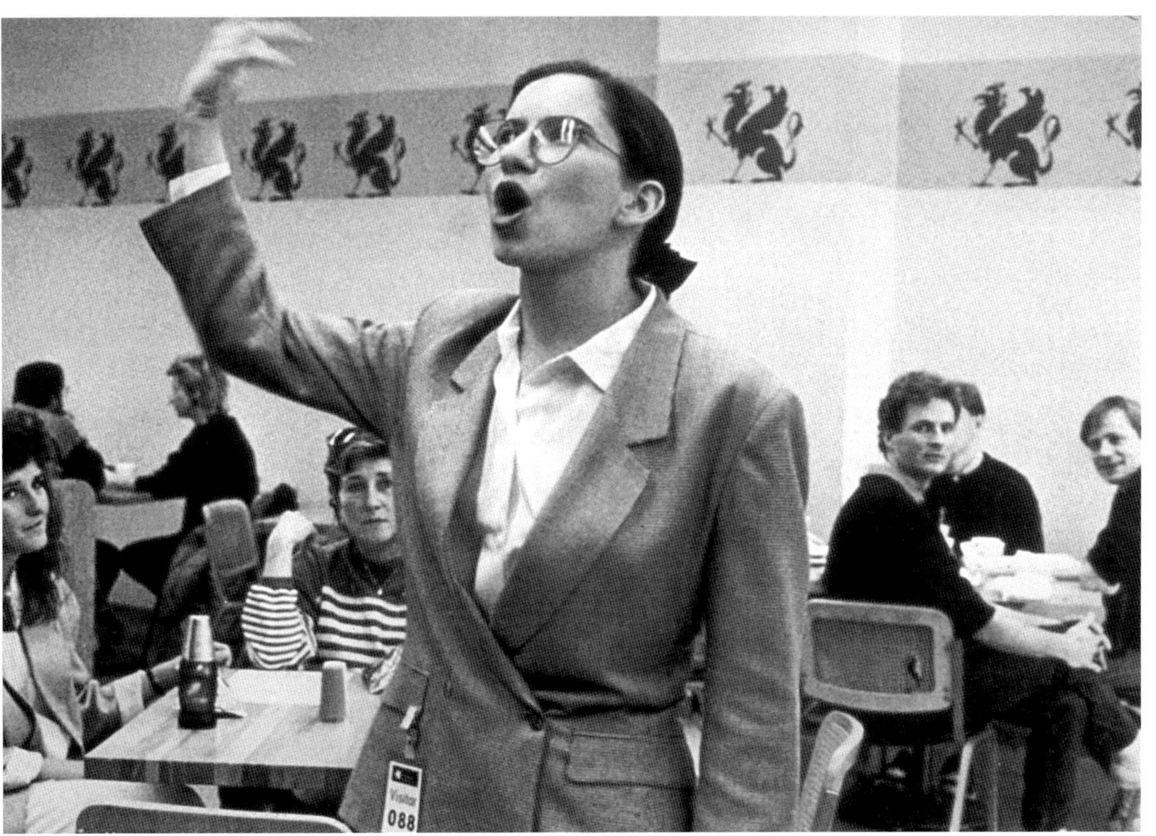

65

virtual spaces in the metaverse.[29] The works in the exhibition were auctioned on the NFT platform OpenSea. The installation photos look like a physical gallery but take place in this wild, increasingly normalized wormhole of worlds existing inside computing spaces.

Also in 2021, Pablo Rodriguez-Fraile, a collector of both traditional art and NFTs, created Aorist, a cultural institution that lives in the metaverse and which is a lot more than just a marketplace. It supports artists in creating digital creations, which can also live in physical domains, and it bridges the traditional art world and this rapidly developing digital imaginary realm. Aorist spans multiple purposes in order to engage with works that are "richly dimensional" and to democratize access to art. The versatility of what the metaverse is becoming certainly echoes the creative flexibility that Wagenknecht and others are seeking as their practices coexist in the digital and physical even more.

Wagenknecht is frank about what blockchain platforms need to offer, as well as what artists need to question in engaging with this technology. "Depending on the file size, it's extremely expensive to mint [an NFT]. And the proof of work is obviously detrimental in terms of the amount of power and consumption and energy that it

Fig. 7
Andrea Fraser,
*Museum
Highlights:
A Gallery
Talk*, 1989.
Performance
still, Philadelphia
Museum of Art.

needs to generate those hashes. If the environmental part doesn't get you, I think the cost does, for a lot of artists."

Since 2018, she has brought these two realms together in engaging and provocative ways. One example is a series of videos she created called *Self Care and Crypto* that use the structure of beauty blogger "how to" videos to share not only recommendations on face masks, but also advice on cybersecurity and other practical solutions for keeping your identity safe.

> *I was interested in that as an artistic practice. And I realized [also] that the audience [for beauty tutorials] needed this info more than anyone else. A lot of [my] friends who were not at all interested in technology were the ones who had the most to be concerned about in terms of their own personal safety [and security]. The idea initially was that I would hack the ALC algorithms on YouTube by inserting metadata. So, if someone would search for a cosmetic cream concealer, they're going to find my video because I put that in the metadata to essentially train the YouTube algorithms to recognize this as being a beauty blogger video.*

Wagenknecht's work engages structurally with the contours of the technology itself. In the same way that many artists have engaged in "institutional critique" of museums or other arts organizations by reinventing their forms—for instance, the artist Andrea Fraser's *Museum Highlights: A Gallery Talk* (1989), in which she guides performative tours of the Philadelphia Museum of Art that focus on the water fountains or other pieces of museum infrastructure—Wagenknecht is engaging in a kind of institutional critique of technology, reinventing the YouTube tutorial to invite greater participation and self-protection from citizens of an unrelentingly technological world.

DREAD SCOTT

Artists are also engaging with NFTs in politically incisive and conceptually rigorous ways that build on their practices in other media. A key example is the American artist Dread Scott, who produced his first NFT, *White Male for Sale*, in 2021 and sold it at Christie's auction house later that year. This work raised deeply thoughtful and critical questions about the potential of this technology. An interdisciplinary conceptual artist based in Brooklyn, New York, Scott has created a body of work over the last three decades that interrogates the presumed societal ideals of the United States, beginning with his 1989 participatory work *What Is the Proper Way to Display a US Flag?*, which was outlawed by the U.S. Senate and declared "disgraceful" by then-president George H. W. Bush.

Scott's NFT consists of a looped 70-second video of a White man standing on an auction block on a street corner in a Black neighborhood in a urban setting, together with the auction of the NFT itself, which took place at Christie's New York in a Postwar to the Present sale on October 1, 2021. The video locates a White man as a commodity, someone without agency to move or resist. While standing on an auction block, he seems to go unnoticed by passersby. The inversion of history performed in this video is a direct critique of the origins of the United States, whose economic power emerged only due to the enslaved labor of millions of Black people. That the auction of the NFT is ineluctably bound within the work underscores its conceptual premise as a critique of the capitalist system that America built and how fundamentally at odds it is with the notions of freedom and democracy upon which the country was also conceived.

While much of Scott's work has centered on some of the biggest questions about culture, power, authority, and the systems within which such ideas are held, NFTs caught his attention for their purposeful use of the term "fungible." The term resonated with Scott, whose recent work *Slave Rebellion Reenactment* (2019) reenacted the German Coast Uprising of 1811, the largest rebellion of enslaved people in U.S. history. For Scott, fungibility connected squarely with American history and how slavery thrived on the commodification and capital transactions of millions of Black bodies. Connecting with the historical context of the term fungible, Scott identified a much deeper money story:

> *I thought, if we're talking about fungibility, let's actually have a real conversation about the history of this term and, what is capitalism, what is slavery, how are they intertwined? My interest and approach into looking at NFTs was to talk about the social questions that were raised. And then, conceptually and formally, making an NFT that had a physical component of this video, but also that the auction was part of it.*

Scott's *White Male for Sale* pushed the technology beyond aesthetics and innovation to a state of conceptual and political relevance as an artwork and as an indictment of American history. His conceptual exploration of fungibility radically expanded the ways in which the technological underpinnings of blockchain had previously been considered. Conceptually, his work makes clear how interwoven our money story is with our democracy story and provides an urgent call to reconsider and reimagine the possibilities for freedom, collaboration, and democracy that some view blockchain as capable of providing. As he has noted, "When people talk about, 'Oh, [with blockchain and NFTs] we're gonna have more democracy,' I'm like, 'Well, wait a minute. That whole concept has some structural flaws within it that we need to talk about and address.'"

Scott's *White Male for Sale* sold at Christie's for 32,500 dollars based on an undisclosed "estimate on request" to an unnamed buyer. Bidding was limited, and this lack of competitive engagement, as well as the lower price, make clear a

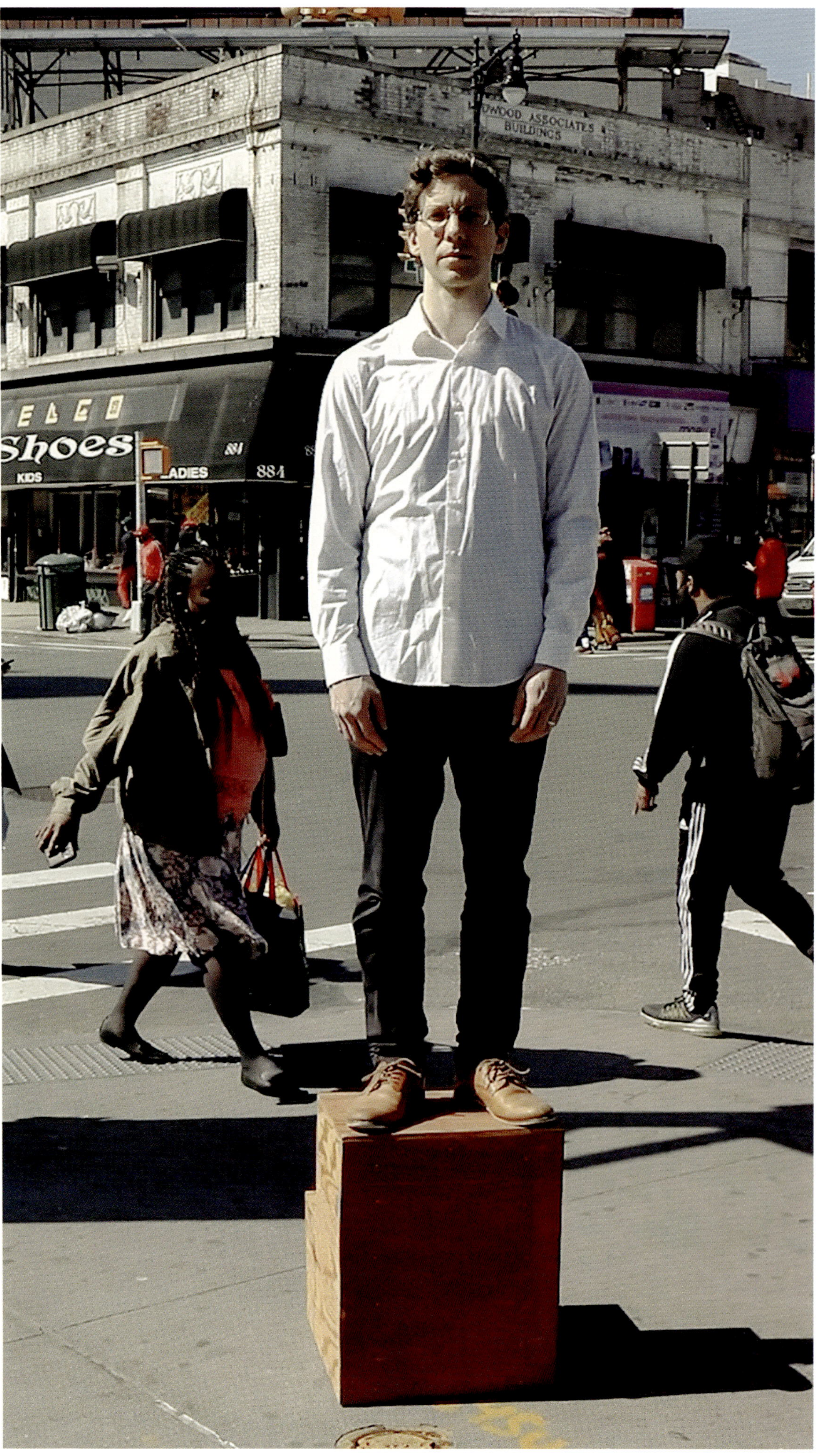

WOOD ASSOCIATES
BUILDINGS
shoes
KIDS
LADIES
884
884

current chasm between the traditional art world and the newly expanded realm of NFT collectors, many of whom amassed early crypto-wealth. Were traditional bidders confused by the technology? Were crypto-collectors uninterested in a socially incisive, conceptually rigorous NFT? Did the work fail to straddle both realms and end up in a space of ambiguity between them? "There's this huge disconnect, even after this racial reckoning of what the NFT space and the people who are purchasing in it are actually buying. [In] a way, because of the lack of bidding and the lack of extraordinary value created, [the sale was] an indictment of the very system [it was participating in]." That the work sold for a relatively low price affirms the system it was critiquing, yet at the same time, had it sold for millions of dollars, the price would have lent additional conceptual and financial value. Scott designed a work in which the monetary and conceptual value aligned, the stories conjoined.

In taking hold of the technology in order to explore the concept of fungibility and its historical relationship to a capitalist economy, Scott situated his NFT squarely within overlapping narratives of art, of democracy, of capitalism, and of technology. With one work, he located the contradictions and contrasting values embedded in these stories, as much as he recognized the ways that the technology can make these visible. In bringing the possibilities of this technology to bear on his decades-long conceptual art practice, Dread Scott created an NFT that exists as one of the earliest examples of conceptual art rooted in critique of both the market and technological structures of NFTs.

NICOLE WILSON

Nicole Wilson included NFTs in a project in ways that engage differently with fungibility or non-fungibility of the individual body and that also attempt, in a manner not unlike that of Sol LeWitt, to set out instructions as part of the piece.

In 2012, Wilson had her body tattooed with the exact tattoos found on Ötzi, a Bronze Age—3300 BCE—man, the oldest known intact mummy. Ötzi died with his dinner still intact in his stomach. He was at once a specific person and an everyman, singular in the preservation and survival of his body. In the original 2012 project, Wilson had fifty-nine tattoos placed on her body with ink made from her own blood. She repeated the project in 2016, when analysis at the South Tyrol Museum of Archaeology in Bolzano, Italy, where Ötzi's remains are, uncovered sixty-one tattoos on his body, arranged in various groupings. In 2021, Praise Shadows Art Gallery in Brookline, Massachusetts, staged an exhibition of the work. With the agreement of the museum, the artist and gallery collaborated with the blockchain company Fairchain to issue the tattoos themselves as artworks. Wilson wanted each work to be

Fig. 8
Dread Scott,
*White Male for
Sale,* 2021. Still.

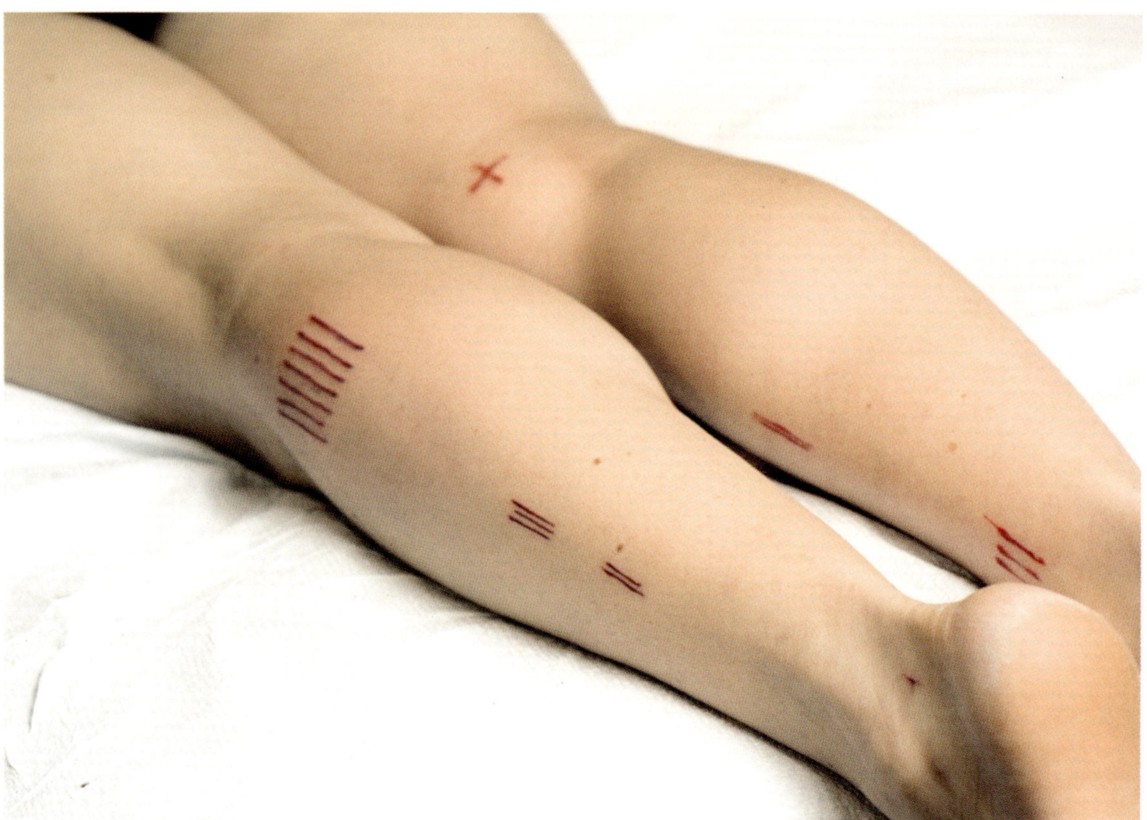

available to people in two distinct ways: to collect as an artwork or to use as a tattoo on the purchaser's own body. Her terms and conditions of purchase, inspired by LeWitt, get at the heart of digital scarcity of NFTs and conceptual engagement with the contracting around the sale of art in ongoing digital form. Wilson's terms and conditions read:

> *A digital file can be purchased for two purposes: collection and one-time individual use. The "Artist" acknowledges that in some cases these two purposes may overlap. She's fine with that. "Collection" is defined as the ownership of, stewardship over, and preservation of the file, including maintenance of the file's security, in perpetuity. "One-time individual use" is defined as utilizing the digital file and executing instructions set forth here by the "Artist" to tattoo the digital file onto the individual owner's body once. Incorrectly collected or incorrect one-time individual use will unauthenticate the digital file. Unauthentication is defined as the voiding the digital file as an authentic work of art.[30]*

Wilson's gambit delicately dances between profusion and scarcity, whereby the work cannot be reproduced in an unlimited manner, but it can be reproduced infinitely, as long as proper permissions are secured in advance. In the same way that LeWitt's wall drawings cease to exist as LeWitt works once their certificates are transferred, Wilson devised a system in which she retains the authority to invalidate the artwork if the collector or user essentially breaks the scarcity of the work—from one to many, reversing the nature of the NFT as non-fungible or singular.

CONCLUSION

Amidst this experimentation by artists—conceptually, technically, and otherwise—it remains to be seen how the market for NFTs will develop. Even as the market has exploded—as cited in the introduction, growing from 4.6 million dollars to 11.1 billion dollars in only a few years—the artist's perspective on that market can be more complicated. And the difference between NFTs created by digitally native artists and those created by artists who come from a more traditional visual arts background is rather vast. The markets supporting these different types of artists seem to be moving much closer together, but the facility with which each constituency inhabits the other's realm remains fraught.

As with LeWitt, artists have made work to circumvent markets but seen that work later commodified nonetheless. In this sense, NFTs both exaggerate the commodification of art and return some conceptual and economic powers to the artists. Especially on NFT platforms that pay artists resale royalties—a topic we discuss in more detail in Chapter 4—artists might participate in markets in ways that do not necessarily need to be commodifying of their art so much as generative of a research and development fund to support future projects.

Fig. 9 Ötzi's tattoos. Nicole Wilson, Editioned digital assets of Ötzi's tattoos, series of 15 framed and editioned digital pigment prints, artist's book, and special edition. *Ötzi*, 2012–2016–2021. Documentation of the process of tattooing with the artist's blood and digital assets of

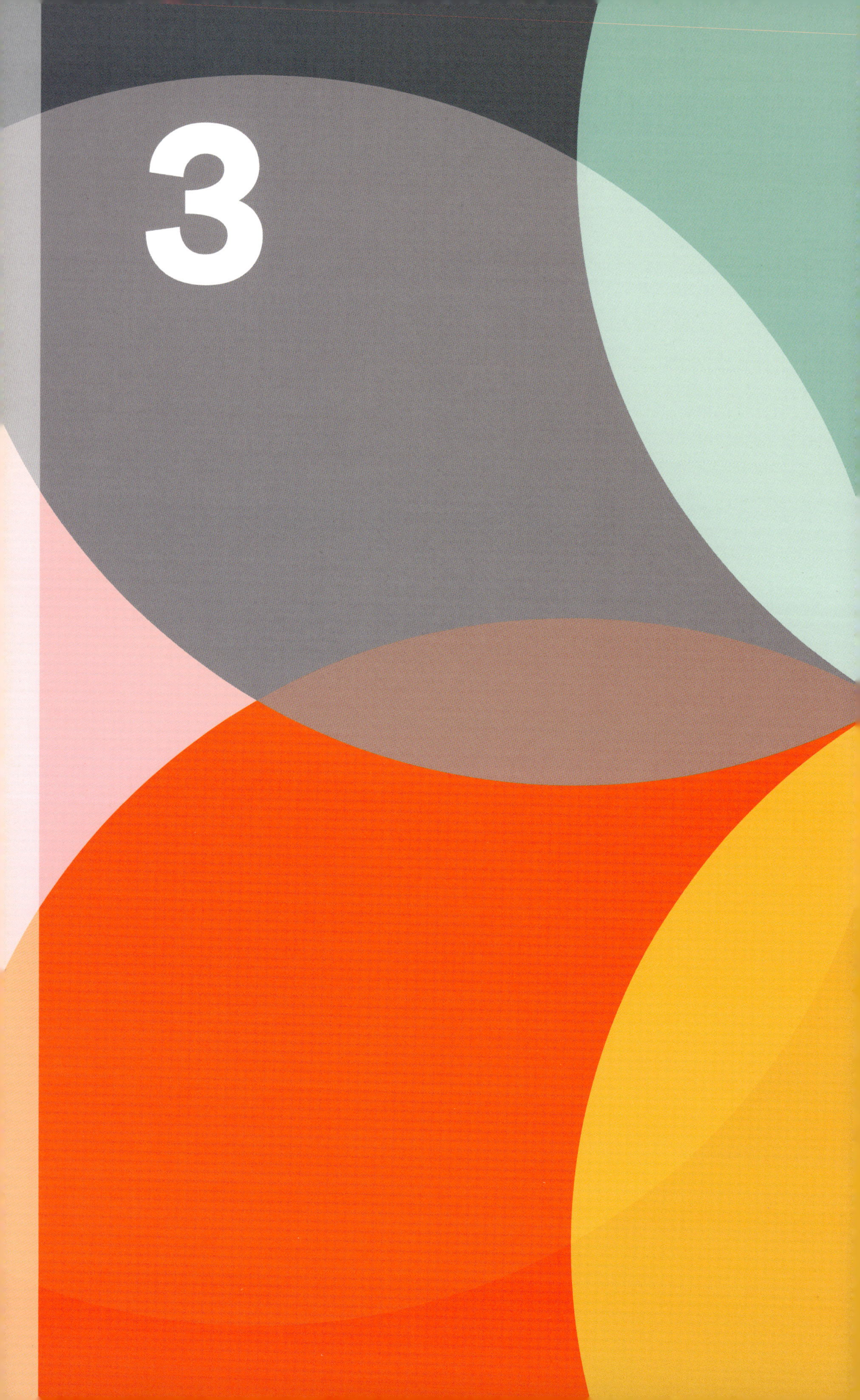

3

COLLECTORS + BUYING

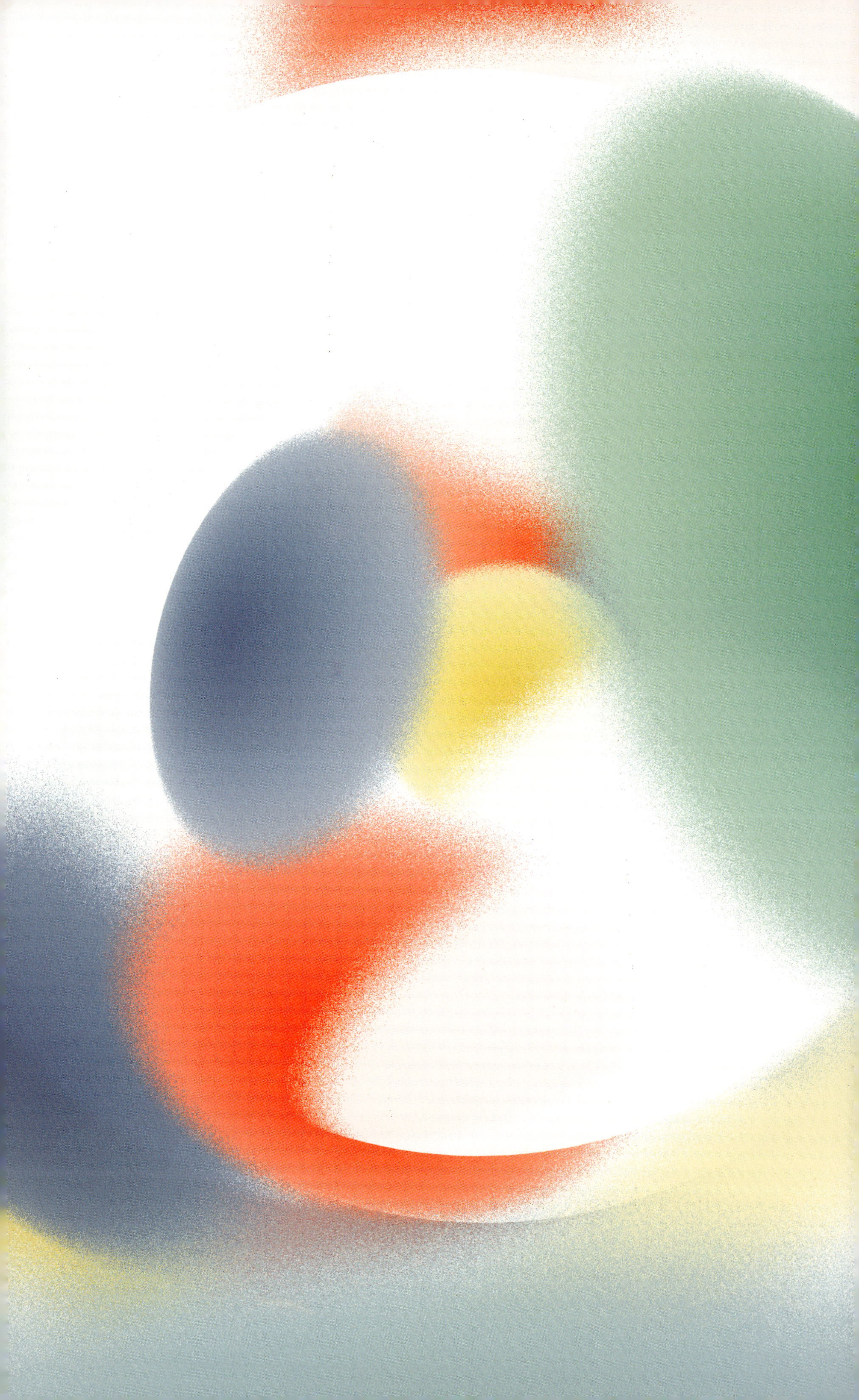

An interesting aspect of this system is that we no longer have any control over the code running CryptoPunks! Once we released it onto the blockchain it became permanently embedded there and can no longer be modified by anyone. This is scary for us as developers because we worry about bugs, but it is also a very powerful feature of the system. It allows a user to verify that there are indeed only 10,000 Punks, check that we can't steal them from you, and basically make sure that everything we told you about the code is true.[31]

—MATT HALL AND JOHN WATKINSON,
CREATORS OF THE *CRYPTOPUNKS* NFT COLLECTION

IN JANUARY 2020, the Rijksmuseum Twenthe, a museum located in Enschede, Netherlands, should have been celebrating the arrival of a nineteenth-century landscape painting by John Constable from 1824. Instead, the museum found itself in litigation with the London- and New York–based Dickinson Gallery, from which it thought it had purchased the painting for nearly 3.1 million dollars. At some point during the negotiation of the sale, the email system used for communication had been hacked and a different bank account was provided to the museum for transferring funds for the sale. The museum transferred its monies by wire to an account

Fig. 1
Dmitri Cherniak, *Transparent Grit* (detail), 2021. Custom software (color, silent), computer, screen or projector (dimensions variable), horizontal or vertical, generative interactive Javascript, GLSL, HTML, CSS Web browser, Linux, Windows, Mac. Edition of 75, one AP.

in Hong Kong—but the dealer never received payment. Questions quickly emerged regarding ownership, security, and governance. Who owned the work? How could that be proven? How could a transaction of this scale not require more checks and balances? These questions were left unresolved.[32]

Transactions of any scale require verification, assurance, and, more than anything else, a system based on trust and transparency. What this case highlights is how, in the absence of such a registry to ensure that degree of openness, trust is quickly undermined and good faith eroded. As artists continue to take hold of the technology, stretch its capabilities, and reimagine its possibilities, the creative once again intersects with the technical beyond production, extending to both ownership and collection-building. The technology story is not limited to the functionality of the blockchain; this story also includes novel and urgent approaches to security, commercial transactions, and provenance. The need for transparency requires a safe environment in which transactions can be performed, in which information can be added—for example, regarding ownership and who retains equity in a work of art—and trusted to be unaltered. Taking a holistic view of how NFTs are collected might help us reimagine the contemporary art ecosystem, including the practical context of regulation, security, and access to that information. The technology story vitally points to the need for ensuring that the other parts of the system—creating, selling, collecting—can continue to operate to the fullest potential of what this technology might enable.

In this chapter, therefore, we focus on what security, ownership, and transparency mean vis-à-vis blockchain and tokenization, and how to harness the technology to ensure a more trustworthy system in which exchanges of goods are clearly noted and communicated to all parties. The fundamental question of buying and collecting NFTs is this: When you buy an NFT, what are you actually buying and what do you do with it? And in acquiring an NFT, what is the process of due diligence? There are three perspectives here: legal, that is, the true requirements under the points of law and existing regulatory frameworks; technical, that is, how the work is put together and securely stewarded; and cultural, that is, what it means artistically to collect an NFT (Fig. 3). We consider these perspectives as a set of kaleidoscopic lenses through which to consider the acquisition and ongoing collections management of NFTs.

It is essential that we define clearly what constitutes a safe and reliable context for transactions of NFTs and also consider how systems around buying and collecting NFTs exist alongside structures of the pre-existing commercial art world. All of the questions around NFTs have analogues to contemporary art collecting. Yet, while the

Fig. 2
Matt Hall and John Watkinson (Larva Labs), collection of *CryptoPunks*, 2017. Algorithmically generated collectible characters and associated non-fungible tokens. From left to right: Top row: *CryptoPunk* 9907, 8066, 8360, 7649. Second row: 3623, 4019, 4346, 4298. Third row: 7079, 7219, 5361, 6255. Bottom row: 2717, 1348, 2426, 0382.

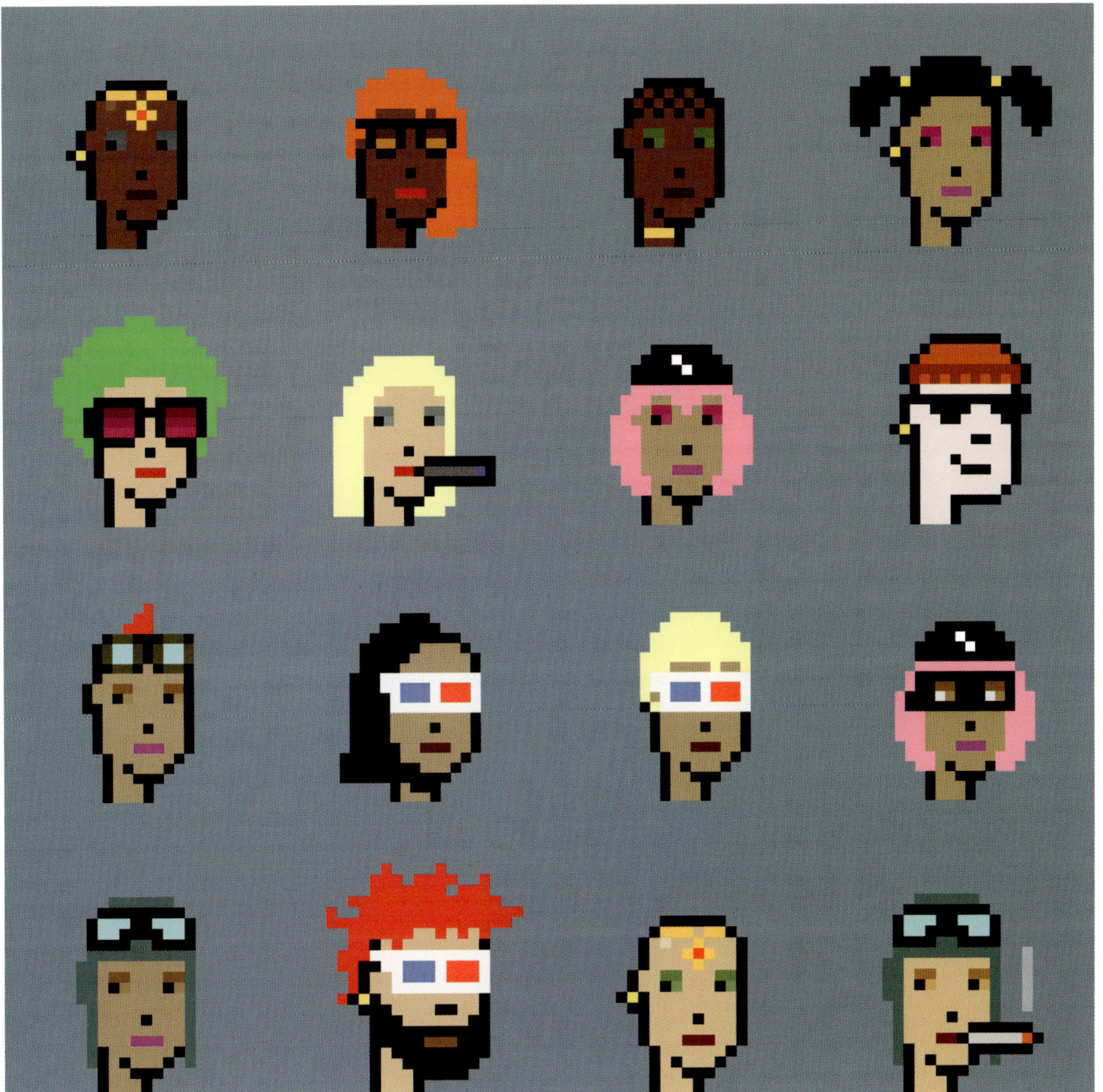

sale of artworks typically involves the informed opinion of trained experts to evaluate or appraise the work in advance, NFTs sell directly over platforms without the involvement of experts in the vetting or evaluative process. Taking a wider view of NFTs as works of art, how does one collect NFTs in depth, and how does blockchain-based artwork live with collectors or collecting institutions like museums? How might one donate an NFT to a museum? Such questions make clear that we are at the very beginning of reconciling the complexity of one system within that of another.

What is particularly poignant about NFT markets is that, in some ways, they show—in compressed time—the arc from artistic generosity to market might that has always been there. The *CryptoPunks* (Fig. 2), a collection of NFTs, exemplify this arc from gift to commercialization. Matt Hall and John Watkinson, friends and principals of the design firm Larva Labs, released *CryptoPunks* on June 23, 2017. Each *Punk* is a 24-by-24-pixel image generated by an algorithm. The algorithm creates heads with different attributes—hair color, helmet, 3D glasses, tiaras, and so on. Hall and Watkinson released 10,000 of them, and they gave them away for free. Anyone could pay the Ethereum gas fee—the transaction cost—to collect one, or many of them, as numerous people did. Not only did they give the *CryptoPunks* away—they also did the creative programming to make the *Punks* the inspiration for the entire NFT standard on Ethereum.

In March 2022, one year after the Beeple sale, Larva Labs announced that the *CryptoPunks* and another project, *Meebits*, had been acquired by a well-known and more commercial NFT company. The sale included the brand, all of the intellectual property rights including copyright, and a number of actual digital works—423 *CryptoPunks* and 1,711 *Meebits*. (*Meebits* are a collection of 20,000 unique three-dimensional characters registered as NFTs.) As part of the sale, the new owners granted the existing collectors of *CryptoPunks* and *Meebits* the same full commercial rights to license or reproduce them that the owners of their other NFTs have. What this means is that a *CryptoPunk* owner can specify how that work is reproduced in the world—from mugs to T-shirts to anything else. While at first the sale may appear to be peak commercialization relative to the roots of *CryptoPunks*, what it actually did was give Hall and Watkinson a research and development fund that they can use to further their other projects and build web3, the new, blockchain-based, participatory vision of the next phase of the Internet.[33]

In 2018, Hall and Watkinson selected twenty-four of the *Punks* and printed them on paper, accompanying each unique and hand-signed print with an envelope—a "paper wallet," or piece of paper containing the private key designating ownership. In June and July 2021, Sotheby's auctioned a group of these ultra-rare *Punks* from the collection of Swiss curator Georg Bak, who had organized an exhibition of the printed works at Kate Vass Galerie in Zurich in 2018. Those works sold in the 200,000-dollar range individually. While those works were sold as part of a special online auction, the *Punks* were also being sold at preeminent modern and contemporary evening sales. The month prior, in May 2021, a bundle of nine *Punks* was included in a sale of twenty-first-century items at Christie's.

What you are buying when you are buying an NFT—a layer cake of rights from exhibition to copyright to enjoyment—varies significantly depending on the terms and conditions that define the sale. This complexity extends from the work itself—whether a property right or a license or just the right to enjoy or the right to commercialize—to the larger context of regulation and taxation. And because NFTs are generally sold online, regulations extend to the arts from other categories, such as Internet privacy, at the same time that anti-money-laundering rules still apply to transactions in virtual space.

We explore below these different lenses and the Venn diagram overlaps in order to provide a more complete overview of how NFTs enter and journey through the world, from conception to tokenization, securitization, potential ownership transaction, and, ultimately, collection. These lenses are evolving in real time, especially as governments struggle to regulate NFTs and cryptocurrencies, which defy easy categorization as currency, security, or other asset class.

The increasing volume of NFT-based transactions brings with it an urgency for building systems that ensure a secure sale of an object. But there seems to be a bit of the tail wagging the dog here, as regulatory agencies and governing bodies have yet to reconcile the different challenges to existing systems with those of the new ones. Finance experts are actively engaged in determining how NFTs specifically might be subject to different regulatory laws and what protections need to be afforded to those purchasing and selling them.

REGULATION

What the case of the Rijksmuseum Twenthe pointedly raises questions around is regulation and how to trust that a transaction is completed in a secure and traceable system. For digital currency and digital objects like NFTs, some key issues are unique to the NFT space, and an increasing awareness of the regulatory frameworks that surround crypto transactions will be essential for anyone considering the purchase and sale of NFTs (Fig. 4).

Such regulatory frameworks may be more recently relevant to the arts, but they are not necessarily new to finance. The main areas that aspiring NFT collectors need to consider relate to AML (anti-money-laundering) laws, which require buyers to be identified and their sources of wealth specified, as well as to privacy regulations such as the GDPR, the European General Data Protection Regulation, which was adopted in April 2016. Even though crypto-based transactions may seem placeless, purchases made in cryptocurrency can have complex tax characteristics as investments (meaning capital gains paid on cryptocurrency gains) and also as transactions, with sales or use tax, depending on the jurisdiction of the sale. We take these regulatory frameworks in turn, spanning knowledge of customers, Internet privacy, and compliance in transactions including tax.

One expert, Sandy Lee, a managing director at a private investment firm and a trustee of an artist-endowed foundation, articulates this condition well: "AML is anti-money laundering [and it] is a good example of where [financial and creative] industries are converging and [now] have to think about the same issue. And regulators have to think about how [to] create a framework that applies to all assets, whether we consider them financial assets or property or cryptocurrency." As Lee notes, in an effort to stave off "dirty money" and ensure that what the Rijksmuseum

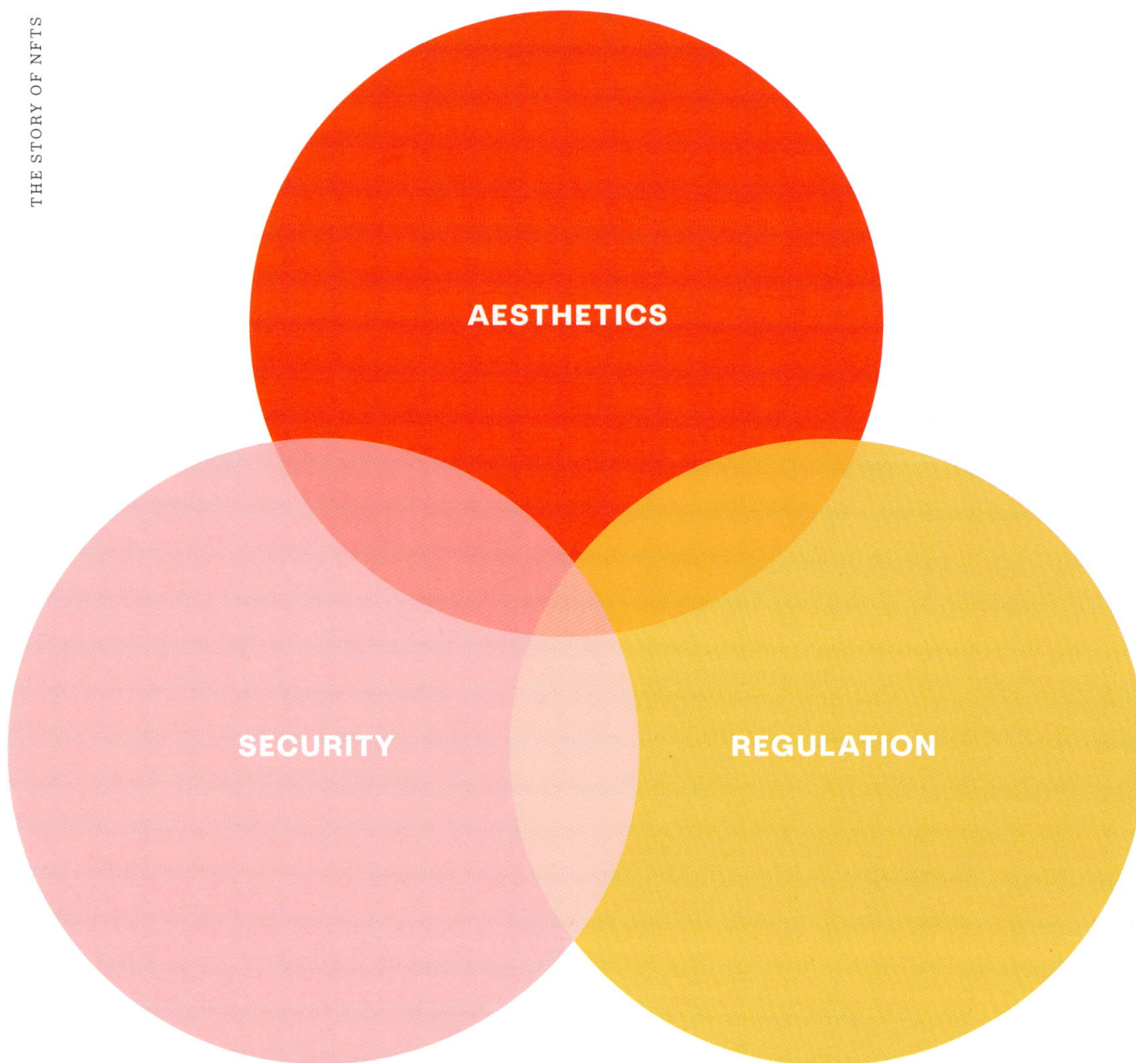

Twenthe experienced never happens again, governing bodies and regulatory agencies are trying to play offense by creating rules and frameworks that prevent the layering or cycling of dirty money into "clean" money transactions.

Sales of NFTs allow for a degree of anonymity that does not meet the requirements of these rules. At the same time, giving this information in an online transaction raises security issues and the potential for phishing. Such transactions require delicate navigation of privacy protection and secure transfer of sensitive personal information, and the standard of knowing one's customer must be met. Nanne Dekking, the founder of the blockchain company Artory and former private dealer and vice chairman of Sotheby's, has spoken about this aspect of trust. His former work was based almost entirely on personal trust, and he originally saw blockchain as a way to replace—or

Fig. 3
Aesthetics,
Security, and
Regulation.

complement—that trust with a system. Artory focuses on blockchain registration of traditional works of art, supplying art institutions with the digital tools to create immutable records of provenance and related research for physical works of art.

Security of transactions is, of course, tied to the technology story and the money story of NFTs. However, decades of commercial transactions in the art world have never relied on transparency, regulation, or "know your customer" types of oversight. The commercial art market has grown and expanded significantly—with estimated global sales growing from 39.5 billion dollars in 2009 to 65.1 billion dollars in 2021—based upon a system of opacity and exclusion.[34] The primary and secondary art markets do not readily reveal pricing, sales volume, or ownership, and the success of this strategic lack of transparency has afforded immense commercial growth and consolidation of market power with those holders of information. As Lee notes, "You see the traditional art market heading toward the need for more transparency, and then on the NFT side, I think there's a debate right now [about] how much information we need to transact, how much information will someone ask for in the future?" Her point suggests an ever-growing tension between the drive toward a more transparent and therefore arguably safer system for transactions, not only for the sale of NFTs, but also for the enduring legacy of privacy or opacity as market power.

This drive toward transparency, especially with publicly accessible blockchain records, is an aspect of tokenization that has massive disruptive potential for the traditional commercial art market. What information can be and should be provided during a sale, and who has access to that information, has bearing on artists, markets, and institutions.

Those with an interest in building a collection of NFTs or even just curious about the mechanics of acquiring one should know that there are additional tax laws that apply to any such transaction. As of 2021, NFTs are still treated as property, specifically as collectibles. If one purchases an NFT with cryptocurrency, the use of the cryptocurrency is itself a taxable event, if there has been a gain or a loss since the cryptocurrency was purchased. According to Lee, "You have to pay the capital gains on how much your ethereum went up in value, and then when you sell your NFT, do you pay gains on that as well? How do you keep all the records?" Thinking through such logistics requires a system of information exchange that can be referenced over time.

Such systems seem necessary to ensure the long-term viability of NFTs. Lee offers a meaningful framing device here: any "move around privacy trends for the purpose of financial regulation—for the safety of the whole system—[can create] a push and pull between how much we want to be anonymous, how much we subscribe to the ethos of decentralized currency and push for anonymity in this, or how much this folds into traditional finance or [commercial] art transactions."

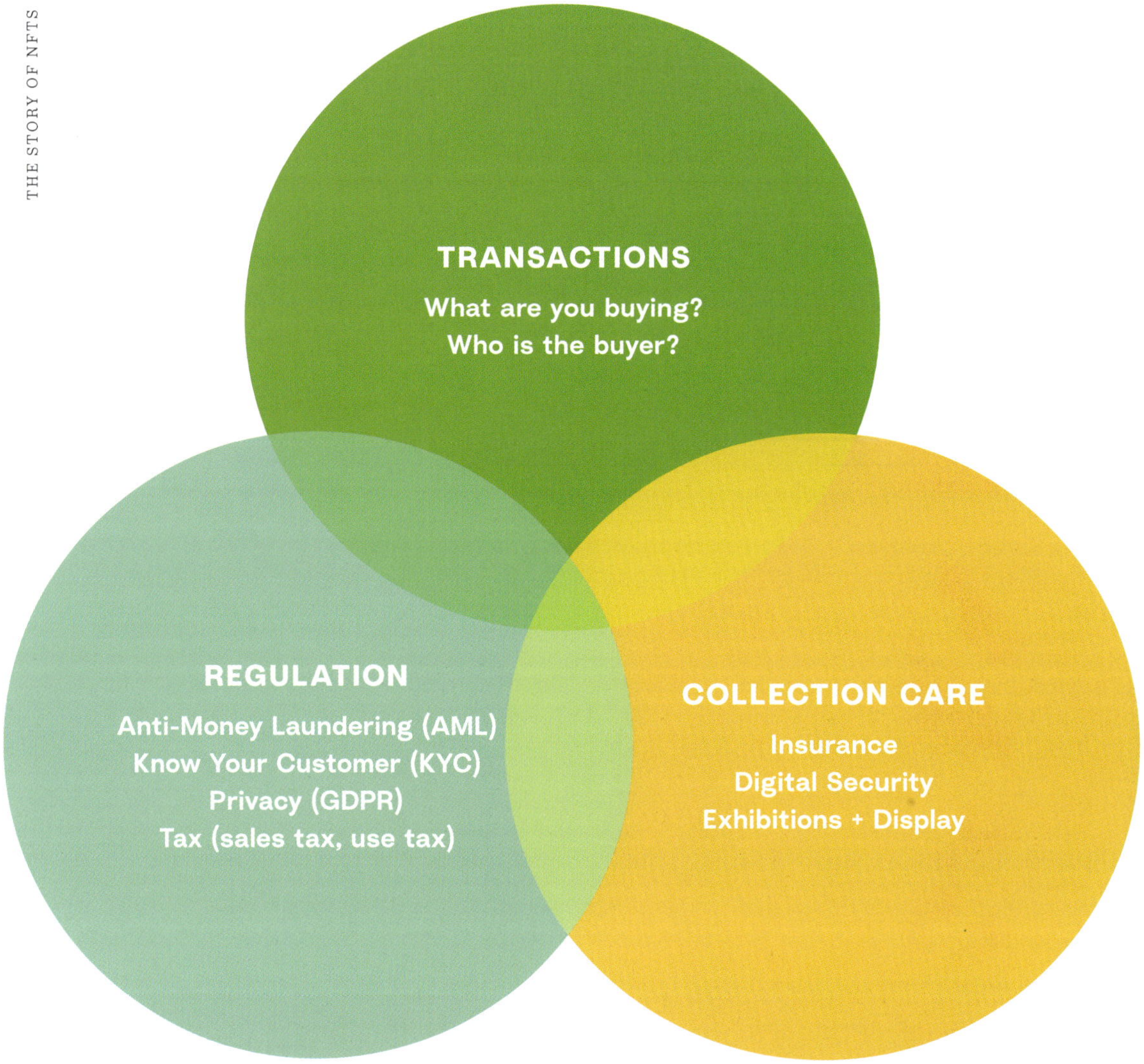

TRANSACTIONS
What are you buying?
Who is the buyer?

REGULATION
Anti-Money Laundering (AML)
Know Your Customer (KYC)
Privacy (GDPR)
Tax (sales tax, use tax)

COLLECTION CARE
Insurance
Digital Security
Exhibitions + Display

Lee's framing of the regulatory tensions echoes the central questions of this book: What happens when the individualistic ideals of capitalism must be reconciled with the collective aims of democracy? Does the move toward transparency aim to disclose ownership in order to ensure the system operates more efficiently or because it's a more surefire way to build trust among participants? Are those necessarily in conflict, or might there be a bridge between the two systems?

The regulatory framework for NFTs is still coming into focus, but what is clear is how the standards of commercial art transactions are also affecting these acquisitions—meaning, NFTs are offering the traditional art world a bridge to a more transparent marketplace. The blockchain affords clarity of information that the art world has historically shied away from in certain contexts. And yet, for art-based institutions, knowing this provenance

Fig. 4
Transactions, Regulation, and Collection Care.

information is essential to collection building. Blockchain invites these as-yet-unanswerable questions about advantages of disclosure or systemic resistance to it.

THE TRANSACTION

While there are numerous digital marketplaces where NFTs may be bought, sold, and exchanged, they all engage directly in the evolving ecosystem of contemporary art. Those new to NFT collecting may find it hard to know what they're actually buying technologically; very few artworks exist on chain, meaning actually on the blockchain, as opposed to stored elsewhere on the Internet with a pointer to the blockchain record. Because NFTs registered to the blockchain more commonly point to digital files, the logistics of file maintenance become critically important. A blockchain record may simply point to a URL that is vulnerable to broken links or defunct websites. Or a digital object to which an NFT points may be saved in multiple copies or maintained securely on the IPFS, the InterPlanetary File System, a more permanent and robust storage system. The work could also be held on a platform such as Nifty Gateway, in which the storage of the work is recentralized to the shared custodial wallets of the platform.[35] These solutions all carry risks or costs. The need to have a reliable and trustworthy system for registering these digital objects, to establish the primacy of one as an original and to dignify it with registration via blockchain, recalls LeWitt's practice of using certificates of authenticity to validate his work as his. Relying on a system that offers validation of authenticity enables an NFT to circulate widely while still having a provenance and a history of creation and ownership that is transparent and irreversible.

THE ARTWORK, TECHNOLOGICALLY

Although NFTs sold via platforms may be directly transferred digital files, many of the sales via auction houses consist of more intricate collections of digital or related physical objects—the "package" offered for sale. Cassandra Hatton, an expert in rare books and manuscripts, as well as the history of science, who formerly worked as a private dealer and is now senior vice president and global head of the department for science and popular culture at Sotheby's, where she has organized many NFT sales, offered some key clarifications. Perhaps unsurprisingly, Hatton likened the sale of an NFT to that of a historically significant collectible or object. When she led the sale of the NFT for the source code for the World Wide Web in 2021, she approached it as a "digital manuscript," an object that only existed in this medium. The Sotheby's sale offered the original code, which included the time- and date-stamps from the code's creation. With the sale, as with other sales of collectibles that have been minted as NFTs, the aim, according to Hatton, was to locate a file and "to declare that there is one true original and mark that with the NFT." As an expert in manuscripts, Hatton was struck by the computer code as a digitally native manuscript, and she noted that the code was "the second most expensive scientific artifact to have ever sold, after the DaVinci codex."[36]

The sale of the source code for the World Wide Web provides a clear analogy of an NFT sale to that of a rare book. A digital manuscript, drafted in code and saved on hard drives or in files, is no less an original than each idiosyncratic copy of the Gutenberg Bible. Hatton's point is that we are looking at original collectibles, even if one is a hard copy and the other in digital form. The terms of acquisition, the value, and the actual transaction do not differ fundamentally for digital manuscripts and NFTs. In this way, NFT sales have parallel roots in digital art, the history of science, and the collecting of rare manuscripts.

Where things start to differ with regard to the selling and acquiring of NFTs is with regard to ownership. A major NFT sale, like all sales transacted through auction houses, requires the most accurate provenance, that is, history of ownership, to the extent that it is knowable. And when one buys an NFT, the digital provenance is preserved via the blockchain. What is important to note, however, is that there can only be one owner at any given time. An interesting development is that single ownership can actually be in the hands of a group of people who have organized as a consortium. We see collectives of people coming together both to create and to acquire NFTs.

On the collecting side, numerous decentralized autonomous organizations (DAOs) are playing a critical role in the market for NFTs. A DAO is a group of people who pool their funds in order to buy a single item that the group then owns collectively. As discussed in Chapter 1 (and the appendix on page 118), a DAO is created by a set of smart—that is, self-executing—contracts. Thus, a DAO is a kind of automated organization or means of decision-making that its members agree upon but that then is executed by the computer programming itself. With regard to the push/pull toward transparency in the marketplace, DAOs obfuscate the collective's individual members. Unlike an LLC, where the articles of incorporation include the identity of each investor, there is no such disclosure with a DAO. As Hatton has noted, and which resonates with Lee's observation about transparency in the marketplace, the function of DAOs is for everybody to be anonymous. DAOs ask us to reconcile new structures available via automated contracts and blockchain with legacy structures of the art market—mapping newer technological forms of anonymity and collective action onto older forms of regulation and norms of opacity around art sales. In addition, DAOs present complications for anti-money-laundering compliance because a DAO does not have one individual beneficial owner.

Once again, the potential impact of blockchain is to create a system of transparency, one that is decentralized and non-hierarchical, by relying on information living on distributed ledgers. It is almost as if DAOs are world-creating, that is, they present a reality of shared ownership and anonymity that cannot easily be folded into the traditional art world—to such an extent that DAOs expose the contours of the art market to new forms of scrutiny. Do DAOs perpetuate a money story that is opaque and exclusive, much like the traditional commercial art market, or do they enable more people to participate in a system and provide equal access to ownership of an asset? The answer, of course, is that they do both. The capitalist pressure to sell a digital asset with the greatest possible value once again bears down on a more democratic ideal of shared ownership.

As we explore more in Chapter 4, collectives also play a key role on the creative side of the NFT market. These collectives engage money stories and democracy stories in new ways, as we will explore in the case of the DADA Collective, conceived by Judy Mam and Beatriz Ramos, which started out as a community of artists, an open space held for creative experimentation and innovation, and became a decentralized community of contributors and creators. Mam's and Ramos' forays into the market—that is, taking works made collectively and curating them to function and be sold individually—is part of a larger experiment in what DADA calls the "Invisible Economy" of distributing proceeds back to the collective. These ideals of shared creation, ownership, and distribution are larger themes of the next chapter.

The technology of NFTs introduces an additional theme: that of fractionalization. In fact, what is arguably the most notorious NFT transaction to date—the sale at Christie's of Beeple's NFT *Everydays: The First 5000 Days*—marked the stunning arrival of fractional reselling of an artwork just after its purchase within the traditional platforms of the contemporary art marketplace.

The Beeple event was remarkable not only for its sale price, but also for the circumstances of its acquisition. As discussed in the introduction and Chapter 1, the buyer, MetaKovan, a moniker for Vignesh Sundaresan, placed the work into the fund Metapurse, which then announced that it would allow the public to buy shares of it. It would seem that Metapurse was aiming to democratize access to art, but purchasing shares is an economic rather than political invitation to access. In addition, the fact that the work went directly into a fund gave a new and peculiar life to the record-setting auction price. The record price became self-fulfilling. The buyer created our understanding of the work's value by setting the price himself through the purchase itself. As with other auction prices, we generally take them as a public record that is assumed to represent an artwork's value. In this case, that price was set by a person intimately involved in the further resale. This notion of an investor being able to set a price in a market would be unusual in a traditional financial setting—where we have the idea of the market itself setting the price—and it is anomalous in the arts, too.

Independent of the spectacle of the price, the Beeple *Everydays* sale is pivotal in raising some of the core questions we ask with this book regarding the collision of seemingly opposed forces: digital versus physical, transparency versus opacity, collective versus individual, and capitalism versus democracy. More broadly, the technological nature of NFTs allows authorship to move from one to many—collective—and for artists to sell directly to collectors via platforms. At the same time, DAOs and the creation of NFT funds move ownership from one to many via collectives that provide a counterpoint to the breakthrough idea of the token itself, which creates digital singularity, where an infinite number of copies of an image can circulate.

THE ARTWORK, AESTHETICALLY

The commercial art world is laden with barriers to access—from museums, to galleries, to artists' studios—that do not yet exist for NFTs. Thus, how do we parse an NFT as a work of art without the more typical, documented exhibition history or critical discussion of the work as is often the case available when acquiring a traditional work of art? For some, the appeal of collecting NFTs lies in not having to deal with traditional expertise relating to aesthetics, connoisseurship, or historical relevance—if you like it, and you can afford it, you can buy it. For others, with such a new medium, new marketplace, and new authors, it may feel like uncharted territory.

The vetting process for artworks has, of course, evolved over time—from the development of the dealer-critic system that replaced the French Academy in the nineteenth century to the pioneering inclusion of design objects in museum collections, such as when the Museum of Modern Art acquired the video game Pac-Man in 2012, under the leadership of Paola Antonelli, the senior curator of architecture and design.[37] The vetting process for NFTs is yet to be as institutionalized. Given the pressures toward community care and collaborative creative practice, it would seem, in part, that such a vetting based on centralized authority of experts would be inconsistent with the ethos of this sprawling and self-directed creative community. At the same time, we aim to establish bridges from the history of art to the historical context of NFTs in order to build a framework for understanding where this technology came from, why tokenization is the next medium to explore creatively and commercially, and why we can apply similar strategies for understanding and evaluating NFTs based on the tools we use for analyzing and valuing contemporary art.

In spite of the additional complexities of NFTs, they still share with contemporary art a reliance on ownership and authenticity as the essential barometers of transaction security and value. An artist has the authority to sell their work, as proven by a certificate of authenticity, and a collector acquires that certificate as part of the sale. But when we are dealing with digital tokens, it may seem more complicated: The certificate may be held by a platform, thereby recentralizing the holding of the record. Or the NFT platform may grant limited—or extended—rights to the piece, a detail only understood through the information burden of reading terms of service. Thus, it is important for standards and common understanding to be developed by the field—by groups of collectors, by professional bodies, and by cross-pollinated conversations across trusted institutions in both markets and museum practice.

As we noted earlier, the basis for NFT ownership is rooted in the structure advanced by artists like Sol LeWitt in the 1960s. A LeWitt certificate is irreplaceable; if the document is lost, then the work ceases to exist. As LeWitt expert Chris Vacchio shared, "The certificate has to accompany ownership. It really establishes the chain of ownership. [The] certificates, much like NFTs, are just a way of making a new form of art able to be saleable." The NFT's certificate establishes ownership of the single idea, but doesn't prevent images or copies of it from existing in the world, and in that way, it allows others to enjoy and experience the work through a copy. Certificates of authenticity are vital to legitimize for a collector the fact that they actually own the work that they think they own.

We are still in the early days of applying contemporary-art collecting strategies to NFT acquisitions, but one place where the digital has flustered the physical realm is the scenario in which a collector has not only acquired an NFT but seeks to donate it to a museum. Such gifts of artwork are a centuries-old practice by which museums grow and build their holdings, and these gifts come with particular security and due diligence requirements. An early investor in cryptocurrencies and early collector of NFTs, Eduardo Burillo serves as a trustee of ICA Miami, where he made the first-ever donation of an NFT—*CryptoPunk 5293, "Priscila"*—as a gift to the collection. When Burillo reached out to Alex Gartenfeld, artistic director of ICA Miami, to offer to donate the work to the museum's permanent collection, Gartenfeld enthusiastically agreed to pursue what the accessioning process might entail. With the museum supportive, the challenge really became figuring out how to enact the transfer of ownership from Burillo to the museum. The work needed appraisals both for insurance and for the tax credit for the donation. Many standard means of appraising works are based on "market comparables," though, and the fact that the NFT market was both newly established and ascendant made the determination of comparables more complicated.

As other museums consider donations, Burillo's promised gift can be seen as a key inflection point in the convergence of the digital and traditional art ecosystems. Strategically, the placement of NFTs in museum collections signals a further legitimizing of tokens as a medium of ambitious collection building. In time, the clear and transparent provenance and authenticity provided by NFTs may dovetail with museum registrarial practice and also help support the regulation of these types of transactions. The ICA Miami gift represents an optimism about the possibility for new markets, new platforms, and new buyers that NFTs

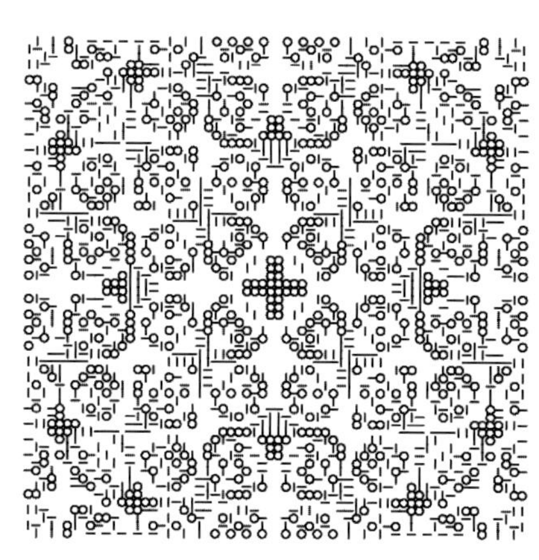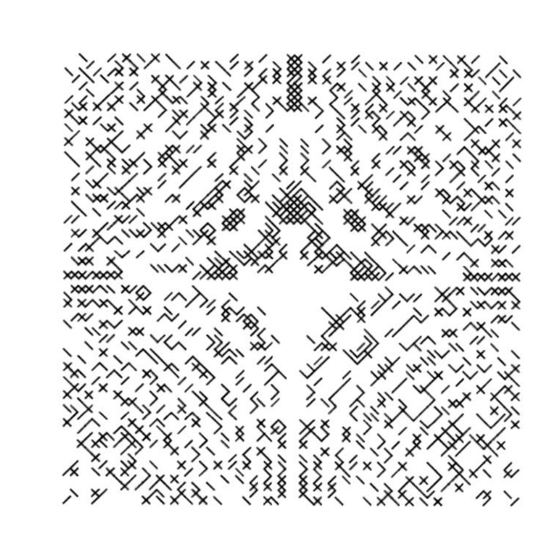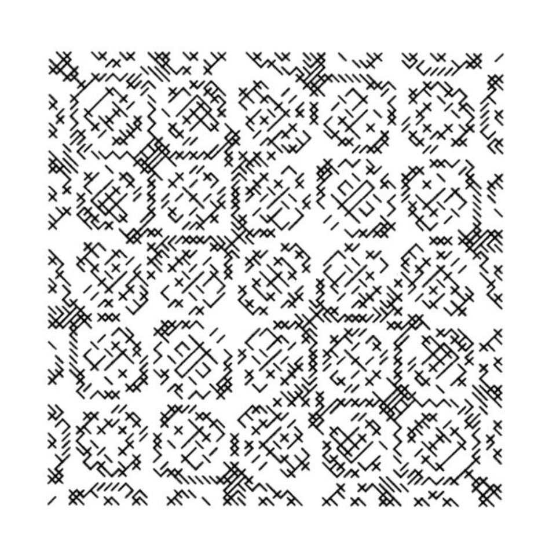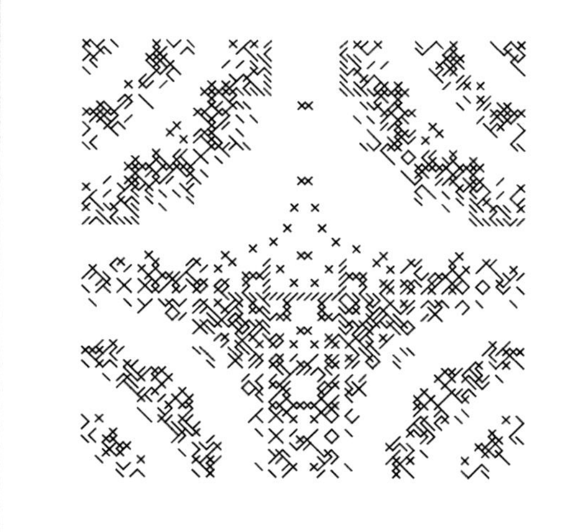

Fig. 5
Matt Hall and John Watkinson (Larva Labs), collection of *Autoglyphs*, 2019, on-chain algorithms that serve conceptually as "instructions" that generate drawings. From left to right: Top row: *Autoglyph* no. 1, no. 2, no. 3, no. 4. Bottom row: no. 5, no. 6, no. 7, no. 8.

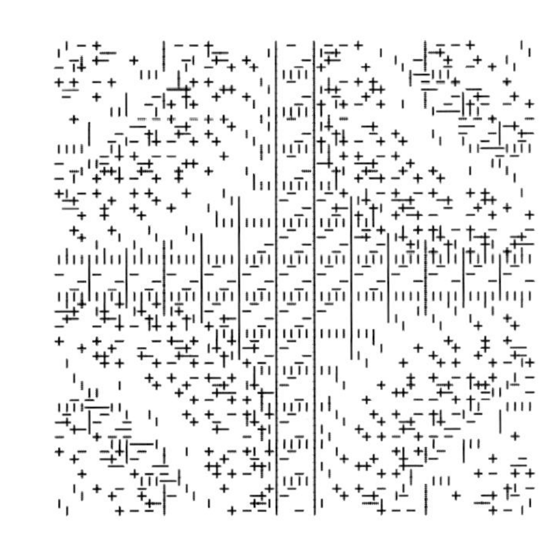
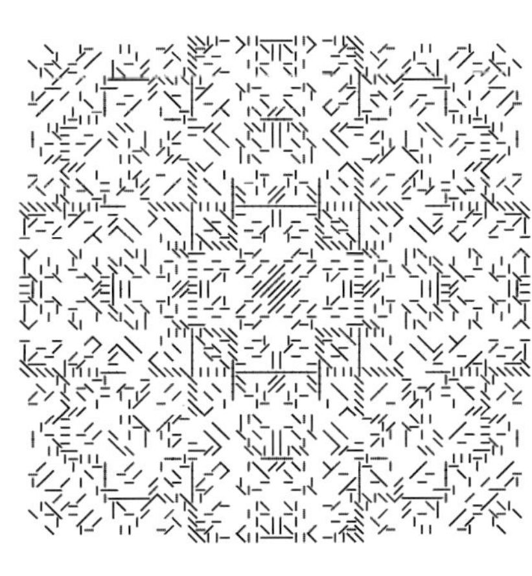
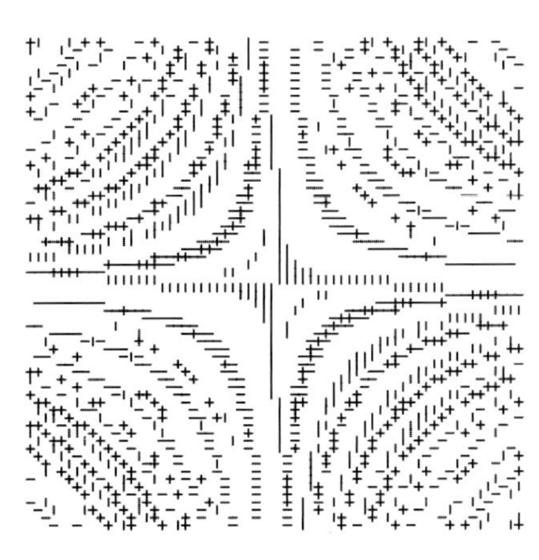
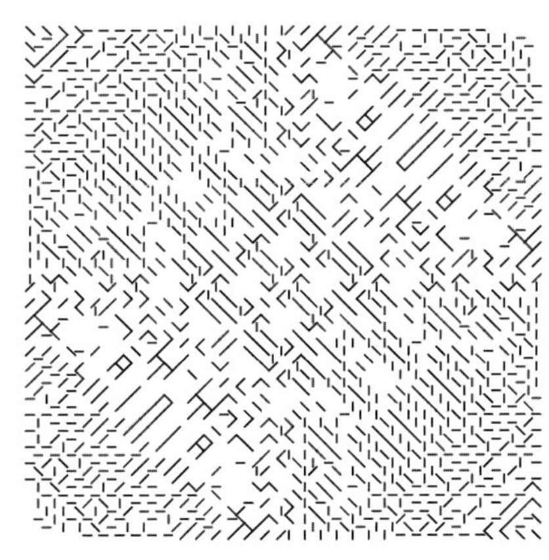

anticipate. It also points to the continued impact of museums—traditional and digital institutions alike—in conferring a curatorial imprimatur.

CONCLUSION

In 2019, Hall and Watkinson, the creators of the *CryptoPunks*, introduced a new project called *Autoglyphs* (Fig. 5). An experiment in generative art, they were the first works to live fully on the blockchain. Hall and Watkinson had been inspired by seeing a LeWitt wall drawing at the generative art exhibition *Programmed: Rules, Codes, and Choreographies in Art, 1965–2018* at the Whitney Museum of American Art in New York. The *Glyphs,* all 512 of them, were created in the manner of a LeWitt: The art was a set of instructions to create a drawing each time. The instructions were small enough to live on chain, implementing LeWitt's famous declaration: "The idea becomes a machine that makes the art." Like the *Punks,* the *Glyphs* were offered free—that is, to anyone willing to reimburse the creation fee (0.2 ETH, at the time about 35 dollars) in the form of a donation to 350.org, the justice-oriented renewable energy and climate charity.

In the *Programmed* exhibition, the LeWitt was installed next to a large work by Casey Reas, the artist and co-developer of the programming language Processing (Fig. 7). In 2021, Reas would found a curatorial platform for NFTs called Feral File. In his curating of the first Feral File show, *Social Codes,* Reas assembled a group of generative artists, headlined by Dmitri Cherniak, whose work *Transparent Grit* (Figs. 1 and 6) became the cover image. The science fiction writer Bruce Sterling posted an essay on the exhibition. Sterling projected all the artworks around his home and lived with them.[38] Perhaps this engagement with NFTs aesthetically is a radical frontier as we collectively struggle to keep up with the pace of development and growth. In addition to functioning aesthetically, the Feral File show would signal some of the themes of the next chapter—the centering of artists, the development of shared and redistributive economic forms, and the ways in which NFTs uniquely connect the multiple selves of a work of art aesthetically, technologically, and economically. The show included ten artists who produced work in editions of 75, plus an artist's proof, priced at 75 dollars.

What is especially interesting about this model is two-fold: First, the artists received 10 percent of the resale price, so they benefited from this move into the secondary market. Second, the artists also received a copy of every work in the exhibition. Thus, if one artist's work took off in price—and Cherniak's has traded in the tens or hundreds of thousands of dollars—the other artists would have the option to sell their copies of another artist's work. The artists and curator owned the artists' proofs and editions one to ten, making sales relatively easy to track, and at the outset it appeared that works for resale were not sold by other artists. More

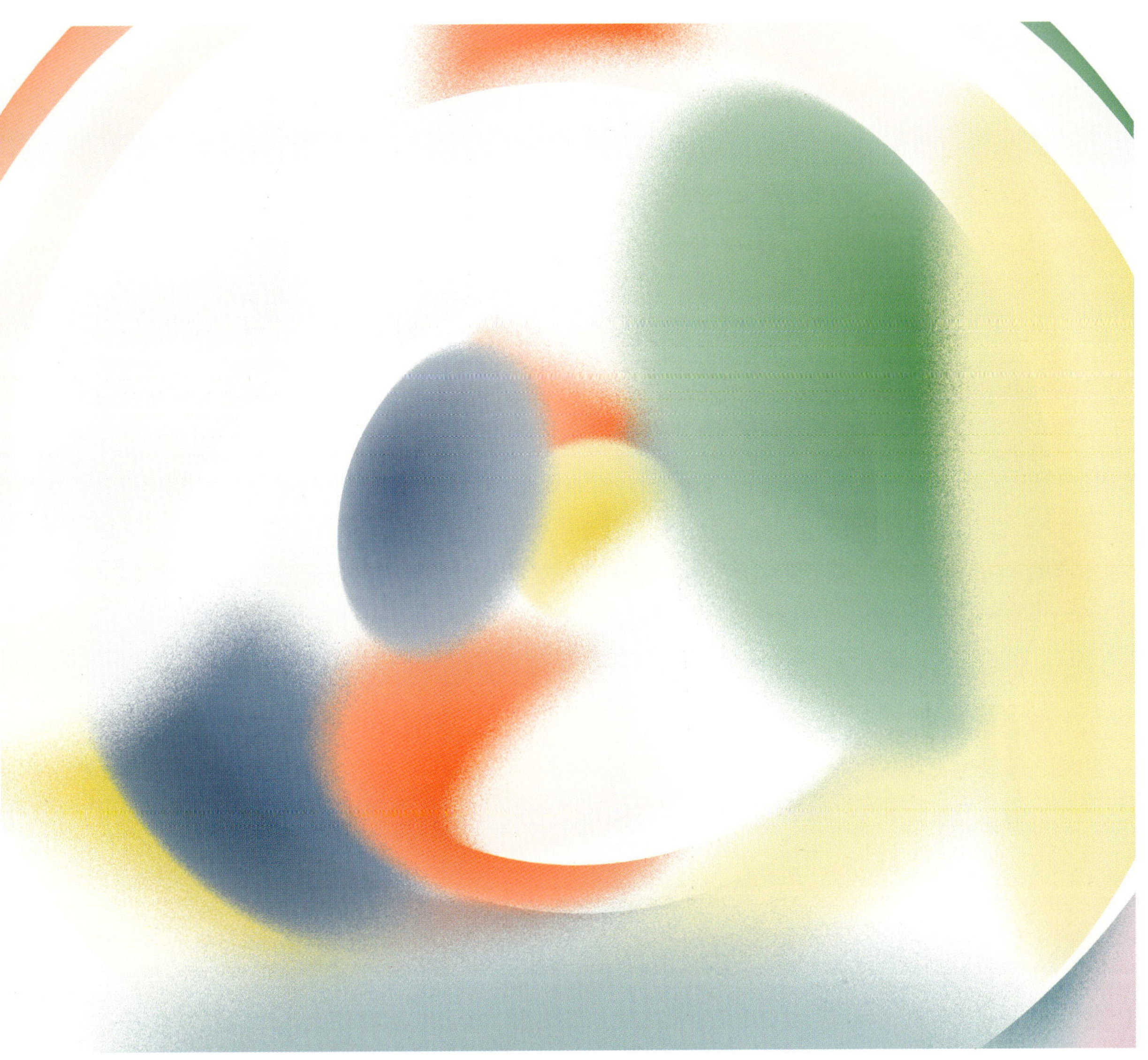

recently, a few editions owned by artists have sold. Many of the resold works are editions closer to number 75, or come from user names that appear to own many works—for instance, one user called "satoshi."

These experiments—and we cover a number of related other ones in the next chapter—start to build new systems. These systems help artists manage risk, they normalize payment of resale royalties through technological automation, and they connect the fate of artists and collectors, creating an arts ecosystem based on shared ownership, with the capacity to change power structures and collaborative alliances in the arts, and beyond.

Fig. 6
Dmitri Cherniak, *Transparent Grit*, 2021. Custom software (color, silent), computer, screen or projector (dimensions variable), horizontal or vertical, generative interactive Javascript, GLSL, HTML, CSS Web browser, Linux, Windows, Mac. Edition of 75, one AP.

Fig. 7 *(following)* Installation view, *Programmed: Rules, Codes, and Choreographies in Art, 1965–2018*, featuring works by Casey Reas and Sol LeWitt, Whitney Museum of American Art, New York, NY, September 28, 2018–April 14, 2019.

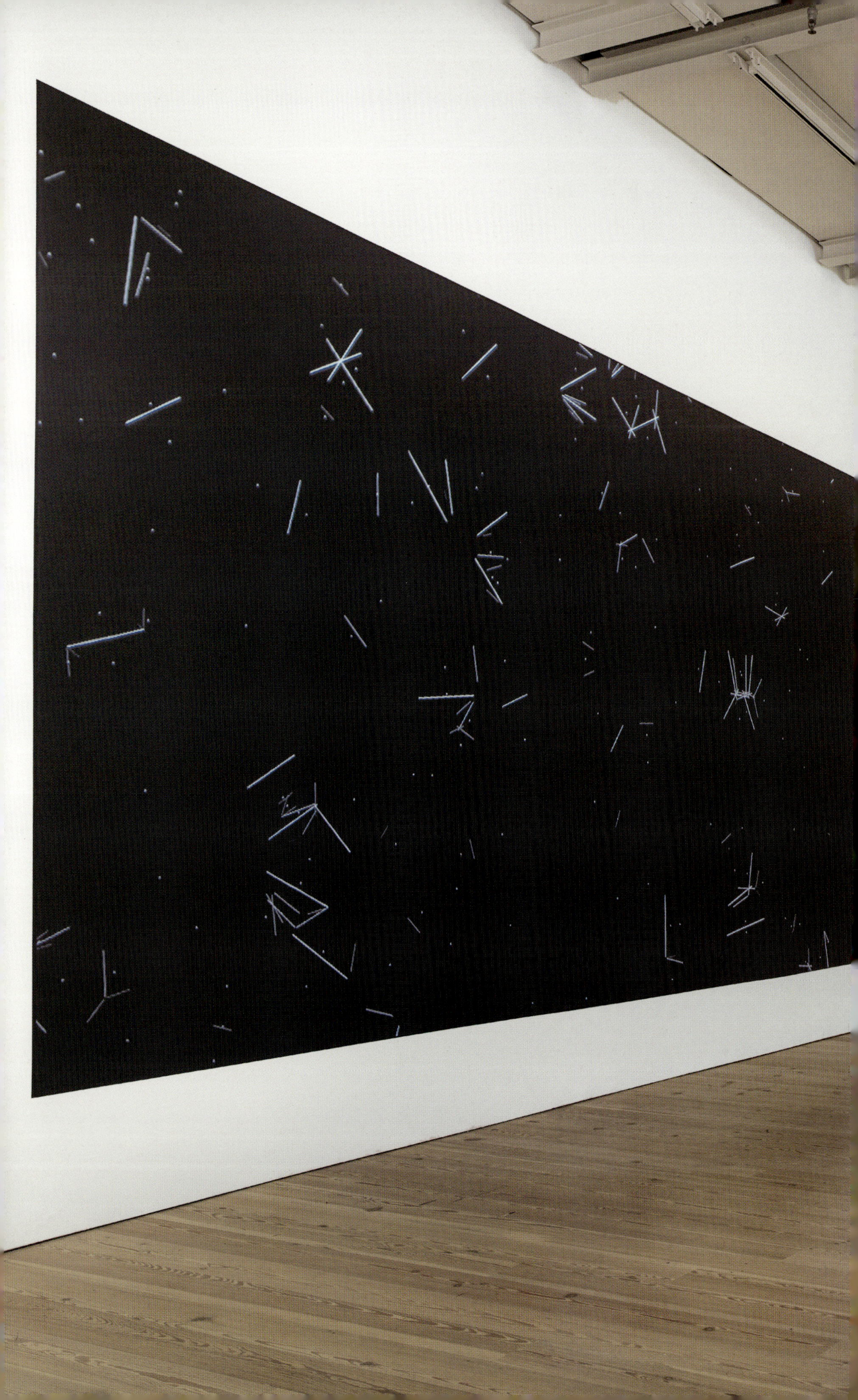

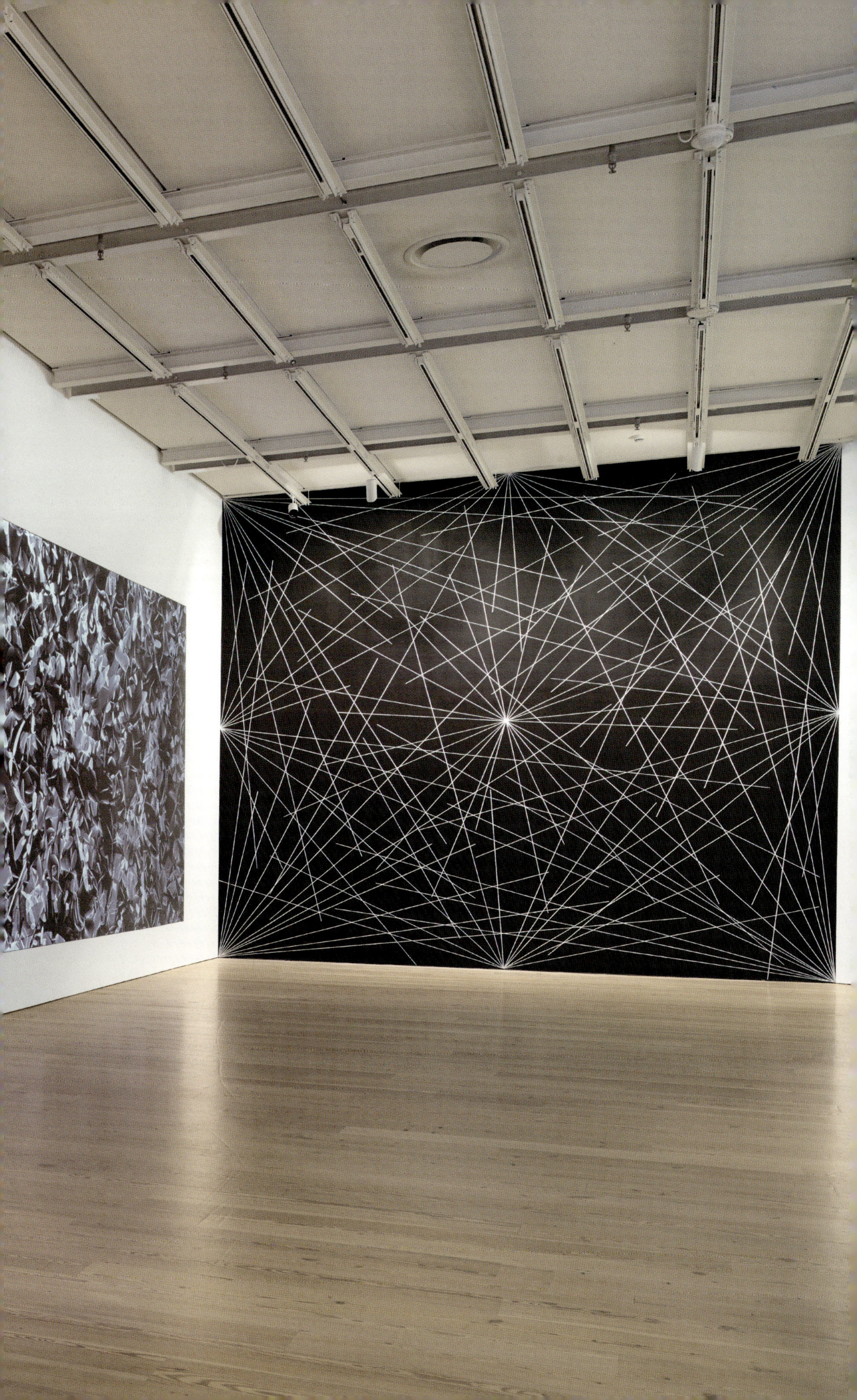

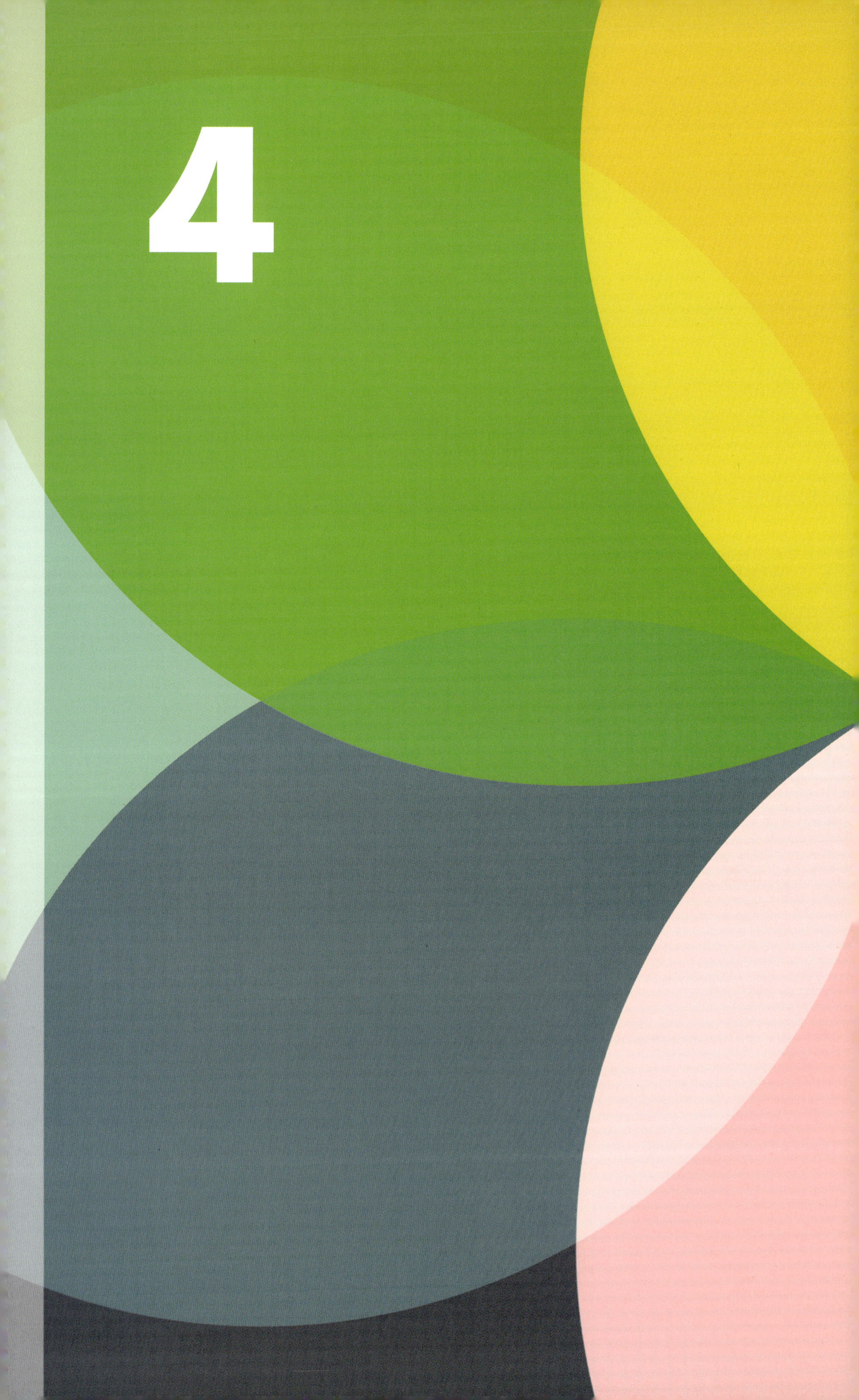

4

FUTURE STATES

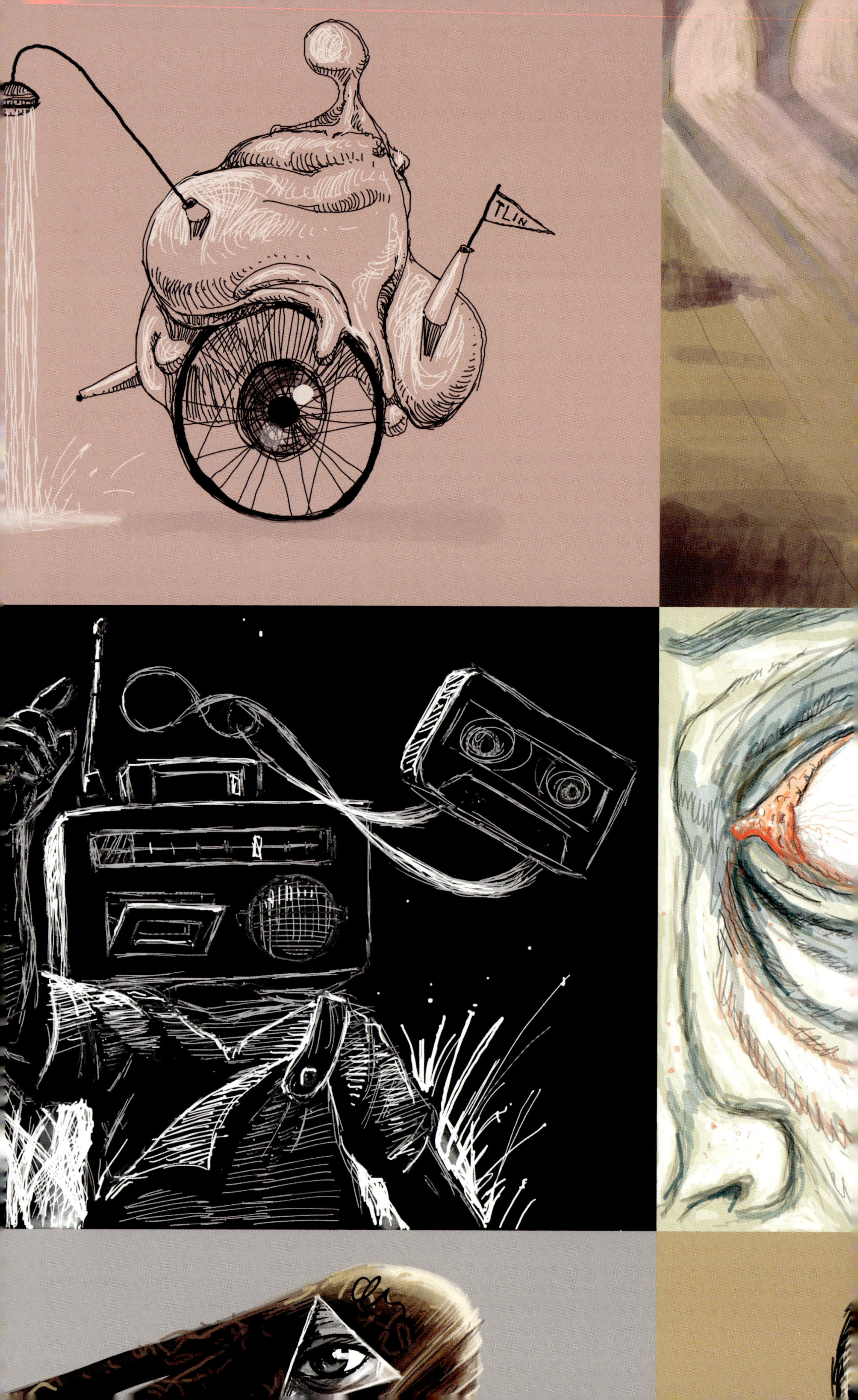

I think one of the biggest ideas that I would put out there is really trying to use and harness this technology to redistribute power—these interlocking systems, whether it's museums, collectors, free ports, auction houses, etc. I also think that one of the really beautiful things is the way in which this technology builds community. That's something that is beautiful. It can be everlasting.

CHERYL FINLEY, PROFESSOR, CURATOR, AND WRITER

BEATRIZ RAMOS WAS WORKING as a commercial illustrator building billion-dollar corporate brands when she and Judy Mam, a writer, began discussing a particular inequity in the art world: Artists built value creatively that they did not own. Artists could put their portfolios online and "people would give you a like," as Mam said, but at some point, as Ramos said, "If we want artists to form a community, we need to give them the tools to do what they do best, which is make art." Ramos and Mam imagined a global collective of artists making work together. The impetus for founding their platform, DADA, was to nurture creativity and to gather people together. To join the community, you had to respond to someone else's drawing with a drawing of your own—to participate in a visual conversation with others.

Fig. 1 *(opposite and following page)* DADA Collective, *Creeps & Weirdos*, detail and selection from the collection curated by Judy Mam and Beatriz Ramos. Minted as ERC-20 tokens in 2017, reminted as ERC-721 tokens in 2019.

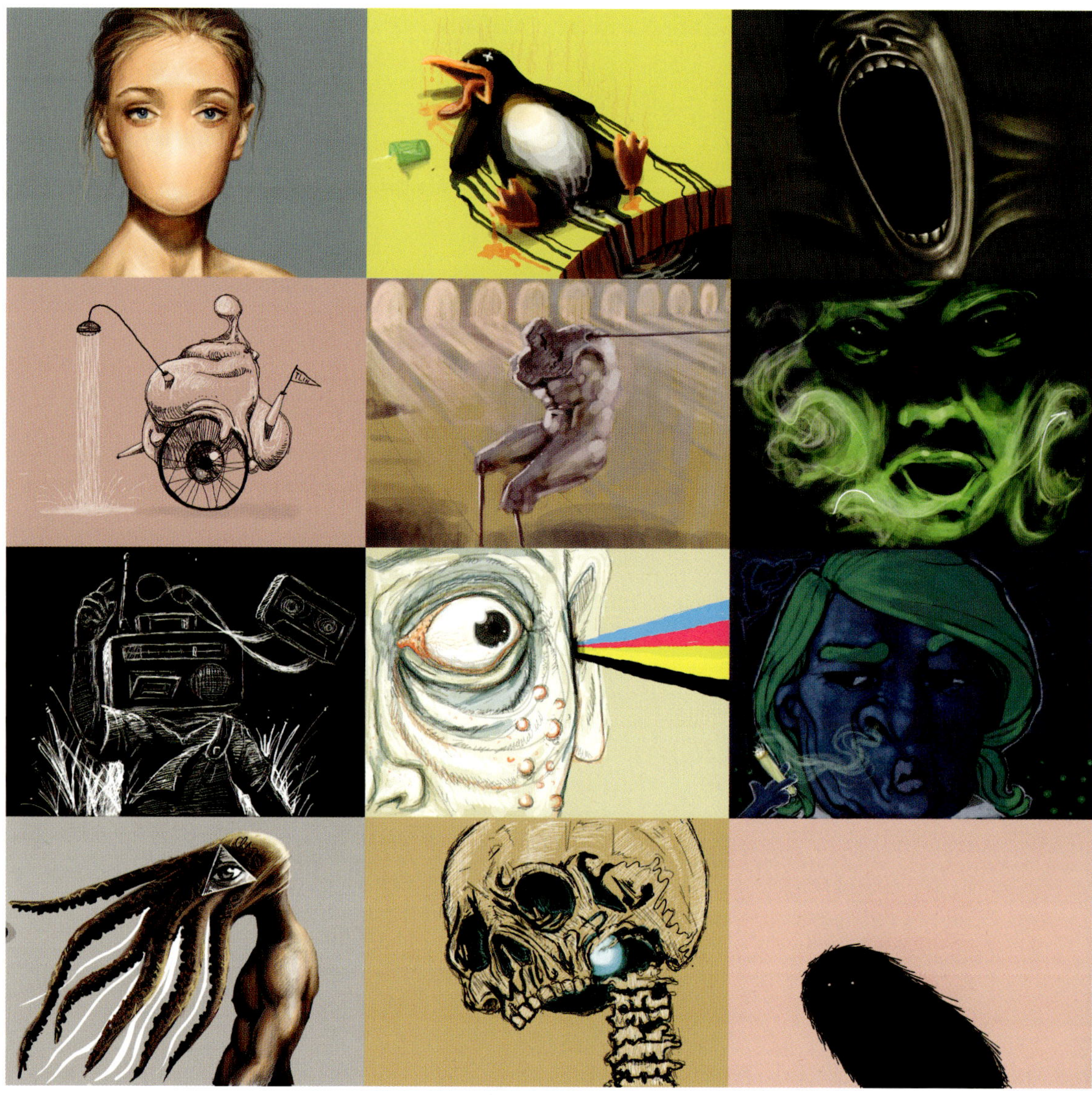

DADA was founded in 2014, well before broader consciousness of NFTs. Mam and Ramos conceived of this digital community as a space where artists could draw, create, and connect with one another. To their surprise, they found that people liked the creative freedom of drawing with strangers from all over the world—not fearing being judged by close friends but experimenting. DADA cultivates not just creative collaboration but also community and does so in part by not functioning as a marketplace. The first DADA collection of NFTs, *Creeps & Weirdos* (Fig. 1), evolved from multiple artists in multiple conversations and was curated by Ramos and Mam. When asked about the title, they said it was because, considering the imaginative forms that these visual conversations had spawned, "some were creepy and some were weird." The name arose from Ramos and Mam's desire to create a "coherent collection to be tokenized." They were aware of the "creepy weird aesthetic" of Rare Pepes, leading them to choose "that creepy, weird aesthetic on purpose."[39] They launched the project on Halloween 2017, which included secondary sales royalties for artists embedded into the smart contract, and have since reinvested monies raised from sales of their NFTs back into their community.

Later, DADA started a different kind of conversation: a series of "Invisible Economy" working groups. They envisioned a future in which art-making could be radically separated from the market and that a shared underlying economy could benefit the entire community from the value created by its members.[40] Ramos and Mam imagined that, although the works could be sold individually, a larger percentage of the sales' proceeds would go into a fund that would be distributed among all the active participants in the community, providing a form of universal basic income. Mam told us, "Although at first individual artists received 70 percent of the primary sales and 30 percent of secondary sales, today all the proceeds from the sales of DADA's tokenized collections go to a general fund where they will be distributed among all the participating members of the community including technologists, according to their contributions." In other words, they organized a collective version of artists' resale rights, the percentage of a secondary market sale that goes back to the artist, in primary and secondary markets.

Within the invisible economy group, finance professor Massimo Franceschet and artist and technologist Sparrow Read studied the platform SuperRare, one of the NFT platforms that had created a secondary market royalty.[41] They asked what percentage of proceeds should go to collectors or artists over time. DADA's pioneering work adding automated royalties for artists also catalyzed a structural change regarding how NFTs are transacted: a group of artists led by Read and Matt Kane was instrumental in the establishment of royalty standards for NFT platforms such as SuperRare and OpenSea.

The questions of this working group and of DADA get at the heart of the political potential of blockchain: Can it create new avenues of support for artists individually and, in fact, create forms of collective ownership, of shared upside, and of surplus that can be reinvested in artistic futures?

We find ourselves in a situation where the world is changing rapidly and we're inside the changing world. As a result, the most critical thing to do is not to answer the questions but instead to try to ask and engage with the right ones. One of these key questions is how these new forms of economic sustainability can come about through fractional equity and resale royalties. A second question is how collaboration and community practice are being built around these systems of royalties and asset formation not just by artists but by other disinvested communities. Here, the questions are not solvable individually, but only by coming together with others. This necessity of collective action may bring about huge shifts in the power structure and huge potential for community governance models.

These questions center the democracy stories of blockchain—issues of redistribution, participation, inequity, and inclusion. While there may not yet be clear answers to these questions, the importance of asking them was the impetus for our series. These questions are the subject of Whitaker's research—and that of many other scholars and practitioners we were lucky to invite in. Our purpose here, in Abrams's term—and image!—is to curate the giant forty-scoop sundae of questions of the future, questions we could never answer alone, but that unite these intersecting stories of blockchain and lay out clear choices for how we choose to design the future.

EQUITY FOR ARTISTS

In 2011, the artist Caroline Woolard convened a working group to consider what property meant for artists. Members of the group looked at intentional artist communities, workspaces, and resale royalties, among other forms of property. As a member of the group, Whitaker became obsessed with resale royalties—the percentage of the sales price in the secondary market that is paid back to the artist. Resale royalties had been criticized for only benefiting artists who were already rich or for not being well enforced. What happened if we looked at them as property? If resale royalties were property rights, they could be traded anytime. If there were a marketplace, an artist could sell a royalty separately from the sale of the artwork. This was both a powerful and a scary idea. It was a way artists might get access to money to make work. It was also pretty close to securitizing the person. As Kevin McCoy said of blockchain, it was one of those new ideas where it was hard to tell if the politics were "really left-wing or really right-wing."

The crux of resale royalties—whether implemented by government mandate or private contract—is that art is extremely hard to value. It is hard to value at any given point in time because we may all disagree over the aesthetic, social, or cultural value of a work of art. Art is also extremely difficult to value over time. It can take time to understand and even become used to new works of art. Central to this idea is a conceptual definition of art as a process of "inventing point B." It was the philosopher Martin Heidegger (and developed in Whitaker's book *Art Thinking*) who proposed a new way of considering a work of art as something new in the world that changes the world to allow itself to exist. Otherwise put, you make a work of art in a point A world, and only in the point B world that the

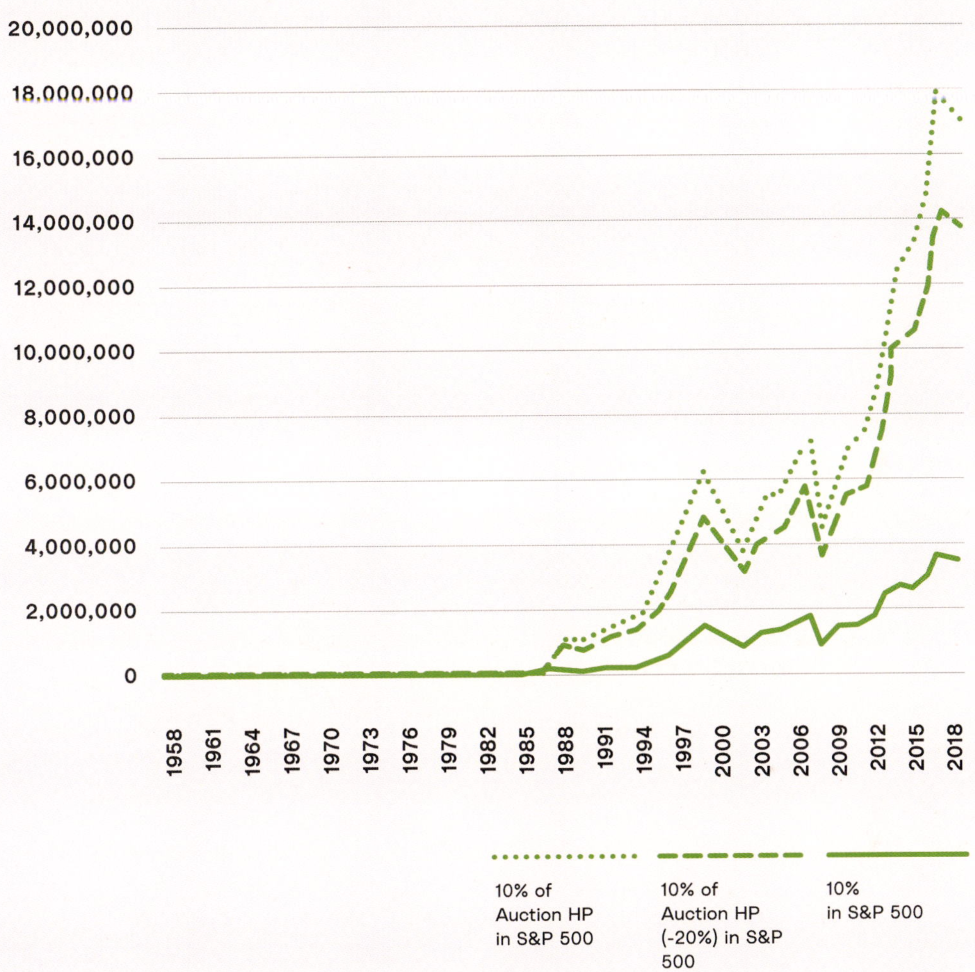

work creates can you know if it has any value.[42] If one looks in archival papers at the sales prices of works of art that now top art markets, one sees they often sold previously for much smaller amounts. A Jackson Pollock painting that might cost into the hundreds of millions of dollars now cost 300 dollars in 1950.

The property group convened by Woolard published a book—with artists Michael Mandiberg, William Powhida, Pablo Helguera, Whitaker, and Woolard.[43] Shortly after the book's publication, Whitaker learned about blockchain and understood it was a registry

Fig. 2
Amy Whitaker and Roman Kräussl, *Fractional Equity in Art*, 2020. (Chart shown in US dollars.)

where artists could trade their resale royalties and where such systems of payment could be managed more cheaply and transparently through automation. Instead of advocating for governmentally sanctioned resale rights in the United States, she started to model fractional equity: Artists would buy a share of their own work by forgoing income when the work first sold. Working with Roman Kräussl, a finance professor, to combine these archival primary market sales with public auction results, we set out to model empirically what would have happened if artists had retained 10 percent ownership in their work. We were stunned by what we found. Artists—albeit famous ones whose papers had been kept in archives—were outperforming the U.S. stock market by a shocking degree. For example, if the American artist Jasper Johns had forgone 10 percent of the sales prices of his early works from the late 1950s and early 1960s and retained equity—so that he received 10 percent of the price when the works sold at auction—he would have outperformed the S&P 500 stock index by up to 1,000 times (Fig. 2).[44] Even looking at the entire stable of various galleries—with artists at different levels of success—we found this kind of market outperformance. How could we talk about it as a means of artistic sustainability, to say that artists were not motivated by profit, but simply that the price they were paid when their work first sold did not match the value later realized in markets?

This is a human problem, well beyond the arts, of having to go for it, to go all in, before you have any idea whether you are creating something of value. What if blockchain could help you own the upside if you did? And what if blockchain could help you pool that risk with others and generate surplus that could be shared across the group? What's so interesting is that it is a market idea, but a market idea that syncs up with the solidarity economy, the forms of collaboration and resource sharing that could redistribute power not only in the arts but in society more broadly.[45]

This is a long-standing conversation among artists to share the upside in their work—and also a long-standing conversation across many fields on collaboration and pooling risks, so that if one person succeeds everyone succeeds a little bit. As we will explore later in this chapter, these ideas date to artist activism of the late 1960s and early 1970s and have until recently been explored more conceptually than economically. It is hard to apply tools of markets to artistic practice because art is discovered in a high-risk environment in which artists are the original investors but don't hold shares in the value that they create. Blockchain makes it much easier for artists to hold these shares because the resale royalty is automated into a lot of the platforms. In this way, blockchain can make some conceptual proposals—for artists both to keep proceeds and to share them across groups—more feasible, especially relative to sending faxes and clearing rights through agencies.

What becomes especially interesting is how decisions are made. For instance, how do you decide how to distribute the surplus? Do all the artist members vote equally, is a central administrator introduced, or are there creative interventions to enhance the decision-making power of those who have previously been the most disinvested? These questions bring a quality of artistic imagination to the economic design around art. The economic forms are in active movement and engagement. The outcome could be better economic sustainability for artists, but also changes in decision-making and power structures among artists, museums, collectors, and broader communities.

COLLABORATION AND COMMUNITY PRACTICE

As we discussed in the introduction, blockchain is a governance system, a way people come together to make decisions and trust information. This replacement of the central authority and potential for cooperation has serious potential consequences for art museums. Museums have historically operated as the expert arbiters of taste in the arts—collecting works believed to be worthy of permanent stewardship. Many of those works are also intended to be accessible to the public. In the United States, museums are nonprofit organizations with educational missions, and both public and private museums and galleries globally have missions to offer the public access to art. Traditionally, that has meant access to what the museums' curators deem worthy of consideration. We trust the expertise of curatorial practice the way we trust the expertise of judges and the legal system. But what about the other side of governance—trust not in experts but in the idea of everyone being a citizen and voting? Although museums have generally, to date, engaged in blockchain by buying and selling NFTs and entering the space with aims of revenue generation, it is also possible for blockchain and NFTs to change fundamentally how museums relate to their publics by formalizing participation or changing financial structure.

The use of NFTs in museums can be part of a decolonial practice, meaning the broadening and counteracting of histories of acquisition of works through colonial expansion of empire and related outright theft. Blockchain can be used as part of restitution practice to register artworks and to return them to host countries. In 2018, Felwine Sarr and Bénédicte Savoy were commissioned by French president Emmanuel Macron to investigate the presence of African cultural objects in French and other European museums.[46] They found that up to 90 percent of cultural objects from Africa are located outside the continent. The Art and Antiquities Blockchain Consortium, a new nonprofit inspired by Whitaker and her collaborators' research on the subject, advises museums, other cultural organizations, and even market entities on how to use blockchain for restitution.[47] Because smart contracts can be set up automatically and records can be seen more transparently, the power dynamics between colonial and source country can be changed. Smart contracts can also

103

be designed inventively around portfolios of objects—some sold, some gifted, some with cash flow. These alternatives also free up antiquities markets by creating platforms by which private collectors can make reparations to countries, selling works and sharing the benefits with the source country, or, again, in cases where portfolios of objects are concerned, selling a portion and returning a portion.

Museums are starting to use blockchain for fundraising, and conversations are being convened by the Association of Art Museum Directors (AAMD), American Alliance of Museums (AAM), and Association of Art Museum Curators (AAMC). These efforts are likely to become more public in the coming years. But the economics are not clear and may change some parts of museum practice. We talked in the introduction about the difference between the *Mona Lisa* being placed on mugs and *Nyan Cat*, an endlessly available meme reduced to one salable NFT. The question arises of whether museums would ever sell shares in the artworks in their collections as NFTs or whether they would sell something akin to a baseball card—an NFT that functions like a mug or souvenir. The first represents the structural financialization of artworks in nonprofit museums, and the second is a symbolic gesture of support or affiliation with the institution. The relaxing of deaccessioning rules—should the AAMD ever relax the rules again, or do so more permanently—could create space for the financialization of artworks in museum collections via fractional sale, compressing the space between museum practice and markets.

104

EQUITY AND INCLUSION, REPARATIONS, NEW ECONOMIC STRUCTURES FOR ARTISTS

These institutional questions are joined by more contemporary practice, not just of repair work for the past—an unending and difficult task—but of possibility and generativity toward the future. This generativity begins with artists and takes conceptual and activist practices of the late 1960s and early 1970s and places them in technological form. Lauren van Haaften-Schick, leading expert in the Artist's Reserved Rights Transfer and Sale Agreement, a 1971 document created by Seth Siegelaub and Robert Projansky and commonly referred to as the Artist's Contract or the Siegelaub-Projansky Agreement, offers some insight here (Fig. 4).[48] We mentioned the agreement in the introduction as a key part of artist stories—of the blockchain and NFT's potential to change the lives of artists, economically as well as artistically. The agreement has specific terms that give an artist control over future sales and exhibitions, but is best known for its provision of a 15 percent resale royalty back to the artist. The contract covers any transfer of ownership, including by gift or trade, and the 15 percent is on the increase of the value of the work. (Some resale royalty systems simply take a percentage of the sales price, not accounting for whether the work has gone up or down in price since the last sale.) The other contract provisions include rights to approve or deny exhibition, a percentage of fees if the work is loaned out, and protection from having the work damaged or destroyed. The Artist's Contract became the model for Monegraph, the company founded by Kevin McCoy and Anil Dash following their Seven on Seven collaboration that resulted in the first NFT, *Quantum*.

Once resale royalties or equity shares exist, artists can pool them, a topic that Whitaker writes about academically and an idea that artists have proposed for decades. The company Fairchain developed a related nonprofit Fund for Working Artists, into which 1 to 1.5 percent of all sales proceeds go. Fairchain explicitly intended to enact artist Robert Rauschenberg's proposal for Change, Inc. In 1970, Rauschenberg incorporated a nonprofit, Change, Inc., to distribute emergency medical grants to artists. A reimagined version of the program, Rauschenberg Medical Emergency Grants, still exists and is funded by the Rauschenberg Foundation and managed by the New York Foundation for the Arts (NYFA).[49]

Artists can access support through these efforts organized under the umbrella of one company, or can self-organize through a DAO—that is, a set of connected smart or self-executing contracts. A group of artists could agree that a percentage of their sales would go to a common fund that would then distribute proceeds automatically or funded grants on application. Other experiments pool risk and share proceeds across artists in an exhibition. For instance, Kelani Nichole, the founder of TRANSFER gallery, used this structure for artists in an exhibition titled *Pieces of Me*. The project was a partnership with left gallery, founded by Harm van den Dorpel and Paloma Rodríguez Carrington and in operation from 2015 to 2022. Each artist received 70 percent of the sales price of the work, and the remaining 30 percent went into a fund distributed to all of the artists.[50]

Providing resale royalties to artists using blockchain may be complicated in jurisdictions such as the United Kingdom and European Union that already have legislated resale rights paid back to artists. The blockchain-based resale royalties may either double-pay artists or be paid to artists via platforms that are not defined as galleries or auction houses and to which the resale royalty legislation does not apply. Regardless of these complexities, once it is possible to use blockchain for artists to claim resale royalties more easily, then artists can also decide to operate collectively—to share risk across groups of artists or to redistribute a portion of royalties to charities or to other artists. In fact, blockchain may allow artists to pool resources in areas where projects have previously failed. For example, the Artist Pension Trust, a for-profit company founded in 2004 and operated under its parent company, the MutualArt Group, amassed a collection of

Fig. 3 *(page 106)* Seth Siegelaub, draft questionnaire in preparation of the Artist's Reserved Rights Transfer and Sale Agreement, 1970.

Fig. 4 *(page 107)* Seth Siegelaub and Robert Projansky, mockup for the first page of the Artist's Reserved Rights Transfer and Sale Agreement, 1971.

ARTISTS

There is no art without you. There is no art world without you. You have given up rights you probably do not know exist. Perhaps you think that you have freedom in your art. But you definitely have no freedom or rights or controls after you make your art. The art world uses your art the moment it is ~~made~~ public. The critics, magazines, museums, and collectors use your art immediately. They trade their today against your (potential ~~X~~ immortality) Tommorrow.

Because they keep you ~~apart~~ competitive. Because of "quality"

Because you have allowed the sale of your art to be the only way to receive direct compensation from the use of your art.

Question:

1. Would it be possible for you to sell just an 80% interest and possession in a work of art and still retain for yourself 20%, plus ~~aethetic~~ and exhibition control?

2. Would it be possible for you to loan a work of art to a museum for a ~~weekly~~ rental fee? Or a percentage of the gate?

3. Would it be possible for you to receive royalties on books on or about your art?

4. Would it be possible for artists to control museums?

5. Will it ever be possible for artists to even control the immediate environment in which their works are ~~seen~~? Known?

Answer.

DATE N.Y FOR FURTHER INFORMATION

SETU SIEGELAUB / THRU THE FACILITIES AND INTEREST OF

FIRST OF 4 SERIES

PLEASE POST

THE ARTIST'S RESERVED RIGHTS TRANSFER AND SALE AGREEMENT

The accompanying 3 page Agreement form has been drafted by Bob Projansky, a New York lawyer, after my extensive discussions and correspondence with over 500 artists, dealers, lawyers, collectors, museum people, critics and other concerned people involved in the day-to-day workings of the international art world.

The Agreement has been designed to remedy some generally acknowledged inequities in the art world, particularly artists' lack of control over the use of their work and participation in its economics after they no longer own it.

The Agreement form has been written with special awareness of the current ordinary practices and economic realities of the art world, particularly its private, cash and informal nature, with careful regard for the interests and motives of all concerned.

It is expected to be the standard form for the transfer and sale of all contemporary art, and has been made as fair, simple and useful as possible. It can be used either as presented here or slightly altered to fit your specific situation.

If the following information does not answer all your questions consult your attorney.

physical artworks as a pooled retirement fund for artists. The company came under sharp scrutiny when it asked artists to cover storage costs in 2017.[51] Theoretically, it would be possible to create a retirement investment trust using fractional shares or resale royalties (where transferrable under law), avoiding the problem of physical storage of works. In addition, the ability to use smart contracts or DAOs could automate processes that were previously too cumbersome bureaucratically.

Van Haaften-Schick reminded us that some of these ideas, as radical as they sound, were present in the planning conversations for the Artist's Contract, even though they did not make it into the final document (Fig. 3). As she told us, much more transformational proposals were discussed in the lead-up to the 1971 document:

> *An artists' survival fund would have redistributed money from the sale of works by deceased artists to living artists. The idea was to use that money to support studio space for artists and buying materials—even to establish a healthcare fund. So, while a plan like the artists' survival fund and others never came to fruition, and Siegelaub was probably very right in being skeptical about how feasible something like that would be, I'm very interested in how such aims might be reclaimed today. Especially as inequality only grows, this just becomes more and more important to talk about. I think if smart contracts can address some of the technical hurdles in achieving something like that, it's worth exploring and thinking about.[52]*

The pooling of resources—as with Fairchain's Fund for Working Artists or TRANSFER gallery's *Pieces of Me* exhibition—can spread risk in a financial sense. As van Haaften-Schick highlights, these systems are also powerful tools to support equity in the sense of both wealth generation and inclusion. In that way, equity can fundamentally restructure systems of power and redistribute the proceeds of art sales.

Cheryl Finley, the inaugural director of the Atlanta University Center Art History + Curatorial Studies Collective (AUC Art Collective for short), distinguished visiting professor, Spelman College, and associate professor, Cornell University, helped us to synthesize across these questions of equity for artists and the impact of these changes on museums and community governance. In addition, the technology itself allows forms of redistribution that were not previously possible. Along these lines, Art Grayson drew on his background as an engineer and muralist when he founded Ujamaa, a start-up aimed at creating equity for artists of color. Grayson said, "The common theme for me is finding a sense of community, finding a problem, especially really sticky problems, and working on something that is not often picked up by a lot of folks."

At issue is how to operationalize a pathway to very large changes in a way that we can imagine, but also to build toward those futures from where we are now.

Finley contextualized this process as an art historian who began her career on the commercial side as an art appraiser. She told us,

The reason I was catapulted back into the academy is because increasingly— and this was the 1980s and 1990s when I was doing this work—I was the only person who looked like me, the only Black woman who was in the auction room, who often went in and out of the galleries that we frequented or who appraised the collections that were brought out to us. And so, I really wanted to see Black artists represented in sales and in exhibitions. I wanted to see Black collectors in the room. I wanted to be able to be in a position to educate the next generation of students who would do the work of either the art historian or the curator, who also might go on to become a doctor, an engineer, a lawyer, someone in finance who would then go on to actually make the kinds of investments that are needed to diversify this ecosystem.

Finley does this work now, in her role at the AUC Art Collective, educating a new generation of students at the largest historically Black college and university network in the country, serving Clark Atlanta University, Morehouse College, and Spelman College. Finley told us that simply teaching art markets as part of art history is critical. She pointed out how many books on the art market have come out in the past thirty years, a sea change in the field. The role of technology and of markets—and the development of language to connect both to art—creates new possibilities for the study of art history and for the inclusion of many more people in the field. As the Strategic National Arts Alumni Project (SNAAP) has found, 84 percent of art school graduates in the United States are White non-Hispanic.[53] The percentage of museum managers is comparable.[54]

While economics is not a complete tool for transformational societal change by any means, blockchain has the economic and governance potential to democratize access to the arts by removing financial hurdles imposed by the precarity of what it is to be an artist. As Kevin McCoy said, "The question of support for artists—you know, material financial support—I think, is really one of the things that's changing most because of blockchain technology." That material support can change representation in the arts—and can also use the arts as a vehicle for reparations, for the redistribution of proceeds to support those who have been excluded before. It is disheartening that these changes have taken so long and have seemed so intractable, and the question remains as to whether this technology can structurally dislodge those obstacles and help us find a way forward. We can't know that future yet, but have some hopefulness that we may be on the right path.

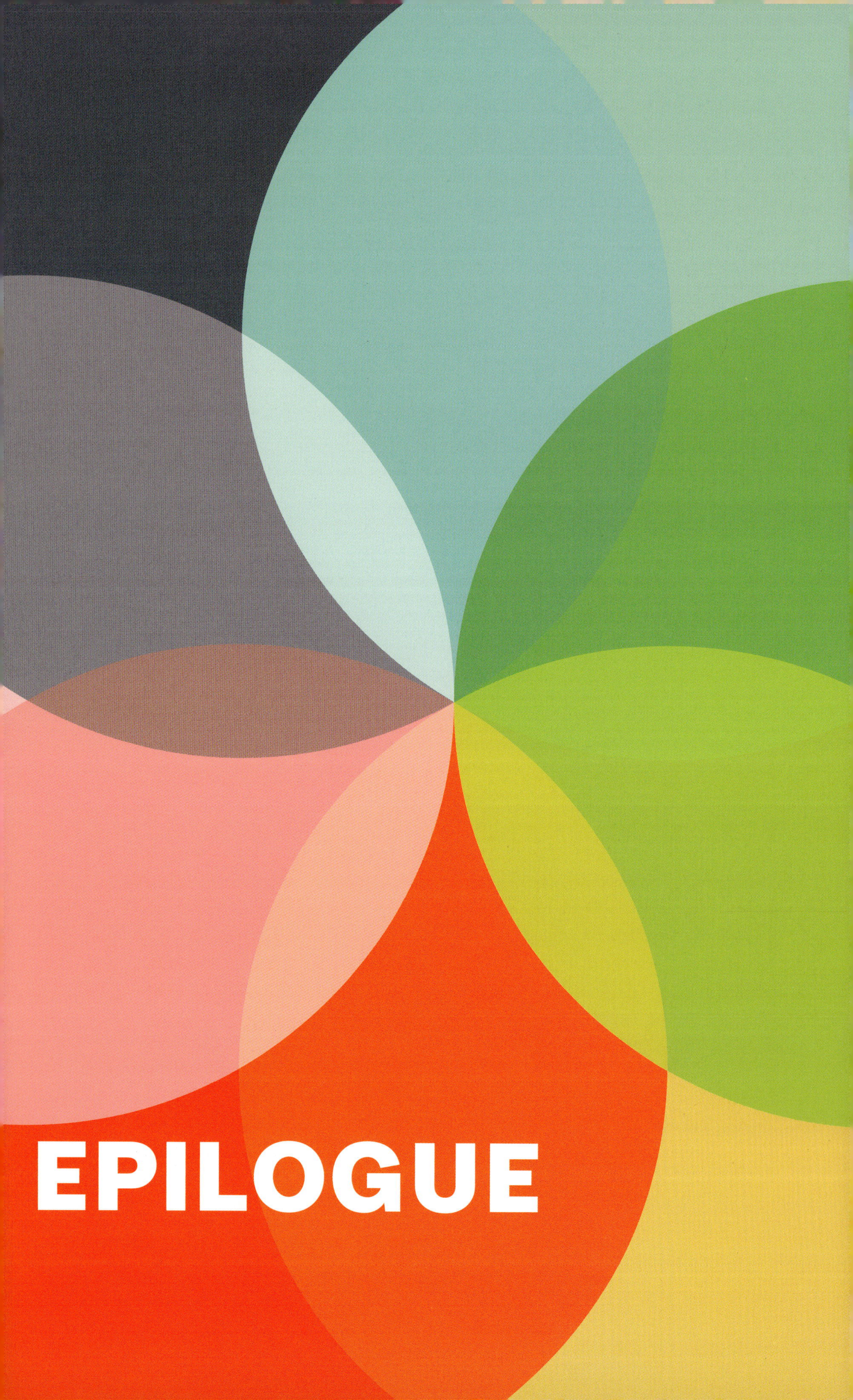

EPILOGUE

What if imagination is what saves us?

—ADDIE WAGENKNECHT, ARTIST

SINCE THE SALE OF Beeple's *Everydays,* the cryptocurrency market has crashed—and may have come back and may have crashed again. We don't know. When Beeple's work sold in March 2021, the price of Bitcoin was, in round numbers, 60,000 dollars. It dipped to 30,000 dollars that summer and rose again to 60,000 thousand around the time we did the MCA Denver program in the fall of 2021 before dropping off to a June 2022 low around 20,000 dollars. Then again, in 1840, the French painter Paul Delaroche saw a daguerreotype photograph for the first time and declared the death of painting.[55] Given how many artists and critics have declared the death of painting in the centuries since, we know that such proclamations' hyperbole relates far more to fear of something new than to the exhaustion of existing structures. Indeed, any certainty about the demise of either is probably vastly overestimated. It is consolation and mystery that no one knows the future.

The way that the blockchain future unfolds will depend on its potential and also its ability to run the gauntlet of existing power structures. It is hard to know whether the crash and burn is the breaking apart of speculative bubbles—including those created by existing institutions with centralized power—not actually related to the fundamental structural potential of blockchain and NFTs. There may be a forest fire–like process of destruction and renewal, or a cycling through and sloughing off of speculation that is noise. Our invitation with this book is to encourage those who are curious to probe that noise, because underneath it are radical new cathedral businesses emerging slowly over time, brick by brick, and new political tools of redistribution and shared value. That structural potential is economic—in creative shared ownership structures, resale royalties, and artists' sustainability. And it is political—in creating publicly accessible, transparent records of information, as well as token-based structures that could be used to enliven democracy itself. The buzzword "web3" is used to describe a wholly decentralized Internet that is based on blockchain and fueled by the same financial powers as venture capital, as well as by collectives of artists and novel structures of a solidarity economy.

We don't know what happens next, only that it is important to live in the questions, and to try to be as clear-eyed, imaginative, and rigorous as possible about the questions to ask. This book is a call to participate, to decide which questions are most valuable and to consider this technology—among many tools—for transformation of the arts, sustainability of artistic practice, and investment in the vibrancy, safety, and equitable future of our larger world.

This book opened with origin stories—with this combination of knowledge and money stories. There was the crypto-anarchist story of motivation to work outside of government, and then the knowledge story of how we will know what was true about the past without trusting a central administrator. From those origins sprang other stories—of the technology, of artworks in the market, of artists' working lives, and of the democratic potential of blockchain. We looked in depth at artists, including those experimenting technologically and conceptually, and then we considered collectors and the complexity of these kaleidoscopic lenses of engaging a new, expansive artistic medium while also being mired in grindy details of regulatory compliance and parsing of technological risks. In exploring future states, we then focused on artists and the democratizing potential of blockchain. It is these last questions—of power and inclusion, of equity in the sense of ownership and also a sense of fairness or redistribution—that ultimately center the artist stories and democracy stories in blockchain's future. To center the democracy story is also to recognize the potential in everyone to be an artist—to take risks and to pursue the unknown—and to draw parallels between the artist and the citizen.

As a researcher, professor, and artist and as a museum leader and curator of artists' stories, respectively, we are unequivocal about the breathtaking possibility of these future states and anxious about how they might bear out. From this place of possibility, we offer an array of questions rather than solutions, in part because we simply cannot claim to know the future—and in larger part because we believe firmly that those who will design these solutions are the creative doers, makers, and problem-solvers who have historically scrutinized our world and reflected it back to us in poignant and powerful ways. This cultural and technological juncture may be no different than some that have come before, but it particularly asks all of us to be citizens, making space to understand the structure of the systems in which we are operating. That invitation is open to any of us.

What will happen for artists? Will they gain power or economic sustainability? Resale royalties, fractional equity, and artists operating collectively could change these dynamics. And what will happen with museums? Will they democratize—will governance become more participatory—or will museum practice narrow? We try to imagine the most radically optimistic or dystopian futures and to consider how we build toward one and away from the other. In this process, where we are navigating the relationship of democracy and capitalism, it is easy to conflate economic participation and democratic access. Buying a share in an NFT can be quite different from being a citizen of the world that NFTs represent.

In recent months, a cascade of artists have announced NFTs, from Marina Abramović to Jeff Koons. Abramović released *The Hero* (2001), a film in tribute to her father in which the artist waves a white flag while riding a white horse, as an NFT.[56] Koons's NFT, titled *Jeff Koons: Moon Phases,* consists of a collection of paired digital and physical works, with a selection of the latter making a moon landing in an autonomous voyage. Koons describes the work's aspiration as to "explore the imagination and technological innovation of the human race." The work is described by Jack Fischer, former NASA astronaut and vice president of Intuitive Machines, as sculptures "documented by the NFTs and housed in a transparent, thermally coated, sustainably built enclosed art cube [that] will be the first authorized artworks to be placed on the surface of the Moon, where they will remain in perpetuity."[57]

At the time of this writing, one of the exhibitions at the MCA Denver is Clarissa Tossin's work on the privatization of space travel and exploration. Curated by Miranda Lash, the show, *Clarissa Tossin: Falling from Earth* (Fig. 1), takes an elegiac look at the history of space travel, casting our current passive acceptance of mogul space flight against a background of hopefulness and common purpose. The Brazilian artist views current attempts to colonize Mars with the moon as a way-station as a recapitulation of colonial histories of extraction on Earth. As if we have learned nothing, we are catapulting private industry into what used to be viewed as a collectively held commons, repeating and not escaping our broken past. To Tossin, what industry experts have called the "second golden age of space exploration" is not that at all.[58] It is the economic colonization rather than democratic exploration of a frontier that was previously considered a global—and intergalactic—shared resource.

As Tossin discussed in an interview with *ARTnews,* our understanding of space has gone from expansive ideals to private ownership in the past fifty years.

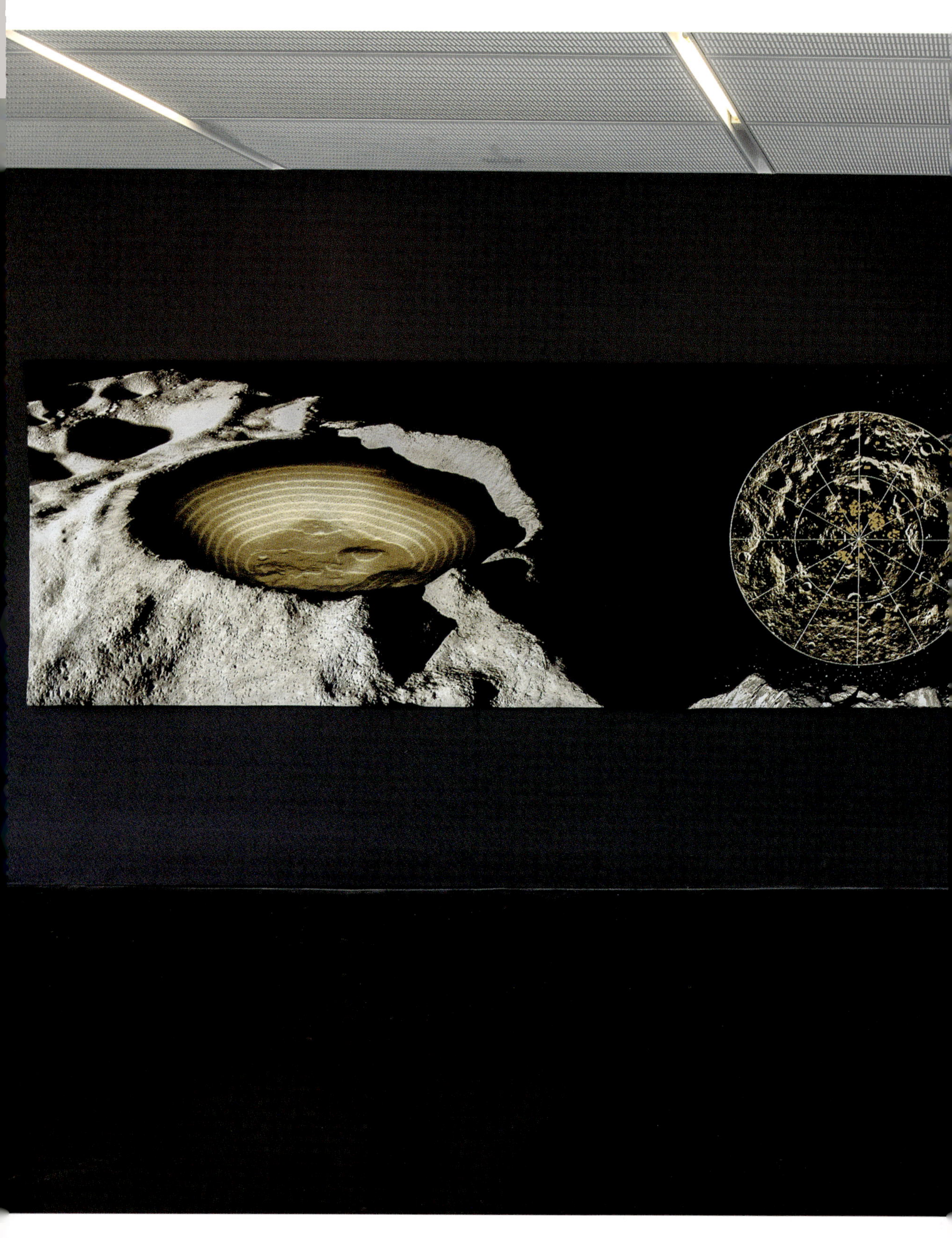

Clarissa Tossin, *The 8th Continent* (detail), 2021. Digital loom jacquard tapestries with metallic thread, 114 x 60 inches (each). Commissioned by the Moody Center for the Arts, Rice University.

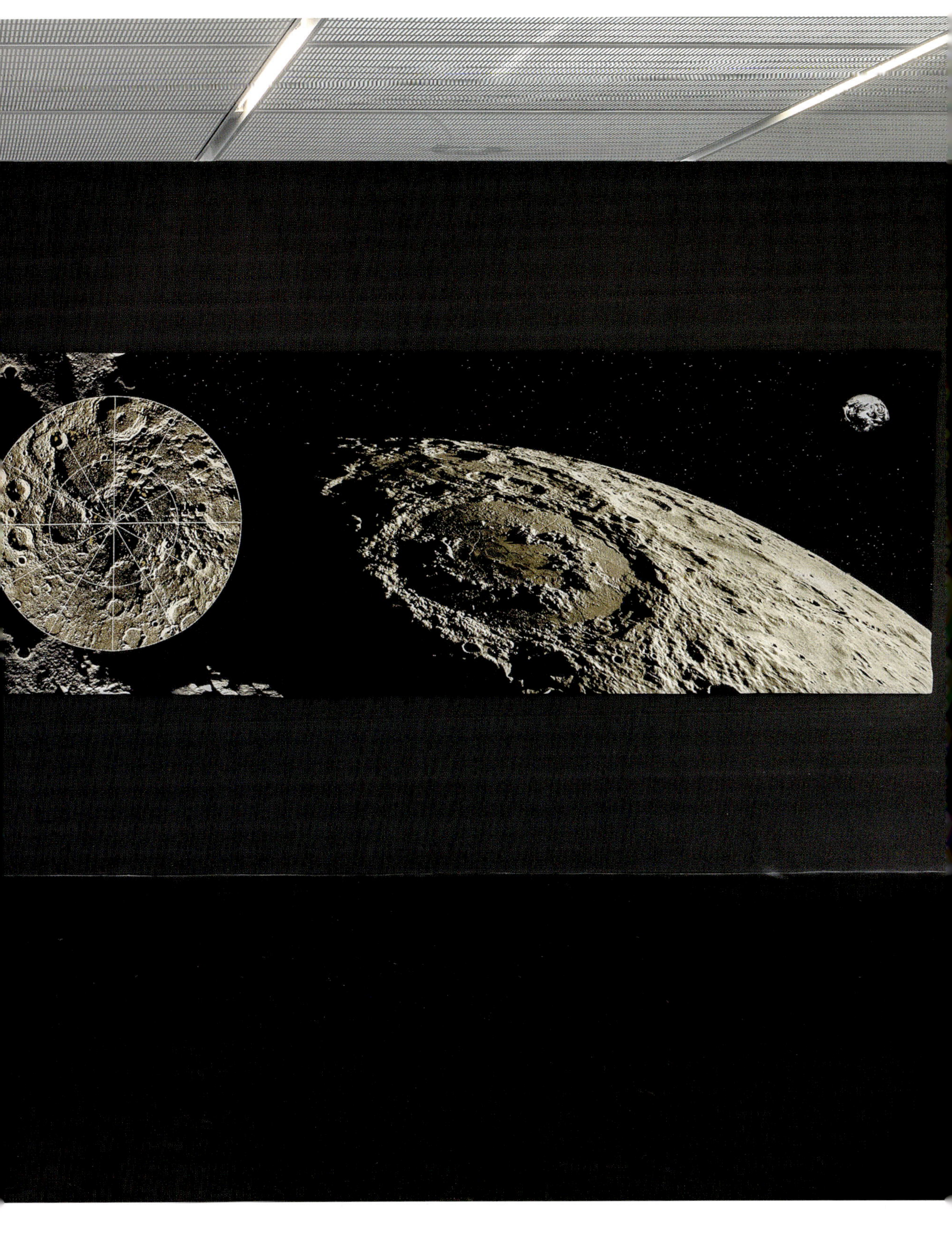

In 1967, the United Nations put into force the Outer Space Treaty. Nuclear weapons developed in the 1950s held the potential to reach space, and the treaty was an agreement instead for peaceful purposes and free exploration of space. The treaty states that the "exploration and use of outer space shall be carried out for the benefit and in the interests of all countries and shall be the province of all mankind." In 2015, then-president Barack Obama signed the U.S. Commercial Space Launch Competitiveness Act, which, in Tossin's words, "effectively legalized space mining by American private enterprise, allowing companies to own mining rights" in celestial bodies, including the moon and Mars.[59] A 2020 executive order by then-president Donald Trump underscored and heightened the encouragement of private, extractive mining of space.

The technologies that we all inhabit already—particularly the Internet—grew out of combinations of public investment, collective shared vision, and private enterprise. It is worth asking how we consider and reassert our shared public life in the midst of privately owned news channels, private exploration of space, and as-yet-unreconciled gaps between private energy consumption and collective climate fate.

We can think of blockchain, analogously to space exploration, as something that could be a publicly owned, shared resource—that is, a way of trusting information, agreeing on a common record or sense of reality, building governance systems that automate decisions we agree on, and registering assets in ways that create shared ownership, even redistribution, and research and development funds for sustainable creative work. At the same time, blockchain has spawned cryptocurrencies, with enormous development of decentralized financial systems ("DeFi") and investment by large banks, venture capitalists, and others who may, in a manner parallel to Tossin's critique of space exploration, be repeating patterns of late-stage capitalism, sometimes under the guise of democratic access, to owning art or otherwise.

The core idea of blockchain—the idea of replacing central authorities and trusting the information without the reputation or role of the record-keeper—is so profound that it would theoretically reorganize society, hollowing out and returning to the people the authority of companies, governments, museums, or universities. It could reorganize nations. This idea is almost without parallel in our more recent history; it is the kind of work of imagining and designing systems that founders of democracies engaged in. It compares to the base layers of a democratic societal design that are so entrenched they become invisible, and yet that are also fragile and vulnerable. Especially as these base layers of many modern societies are called into question, the governance potential of blockchain to democratize the arts and to re-enliven democracy itself cannot be overlooked, whether that potential gets realized or not.

It is our hope that through the simple act of participating in the conversation, we all claim a sense of shared ownership of this technological future and that we consider some of blockchain's ideals and NFTs' possibilities to help us navigate the role of art, the creation of the world, and the pursuit of what we all believe to be of value.

Ultimately the stories of this book are all human stories—stories of individuals trying to solve problems and to strive for meaning and justice, in this case using a new and singularly distributed technological structure. That these are human stories is both the potential and the risk. The technology that replaces trust does not replace community. And it is in that community that we hold the set of rigorous questions that lie in front of us, that all of us are invited to—and compelled to—try to answer together.

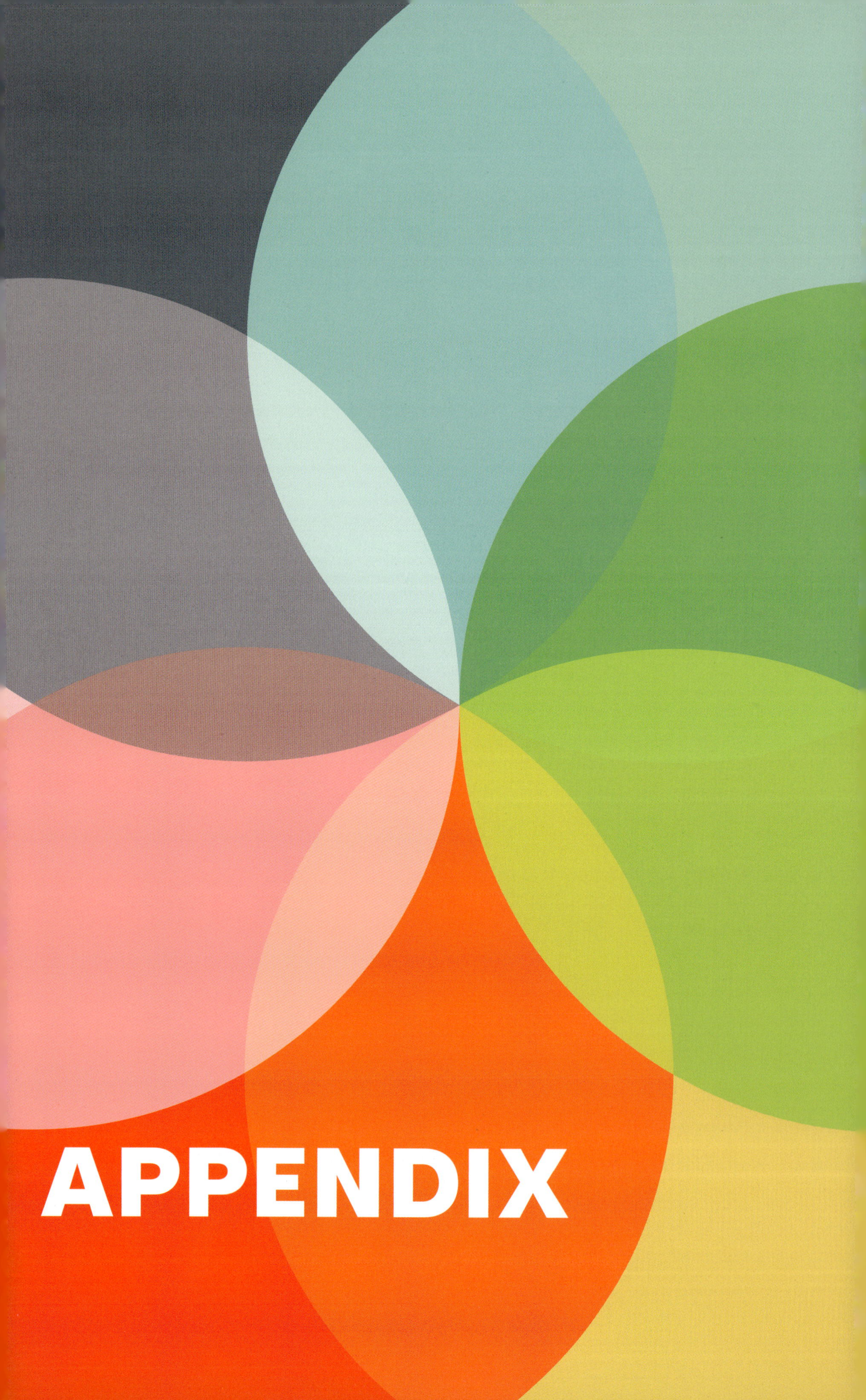
APPENDIX

THE PURPOSE OF THIS APPENDIX is to try to make blockchain and the details of it—defining the platforms and protocols, wallets, private keys, smart contracts—more concrete by going through how an NFT is minted. To mint an NFT is to list an object—an artwork, a photograph, a text, anything—with a unique digital identifier on a blockchain.

Protocols

The first step is to choose the blockchain protocol. In general, blockchain is a distributed ledger, meaning it is a record that is kept across an interconnected set of computer nodes, instead of being managed by a central administrator. In choosing a protocol, you might consider whether it uses Proof of Work or Proof of Stake (as described on pages 37–39), the latter having a lower environmental cost. Bitcoin and Ethereum are the most established protocols. Tezos, Solana, Algorand, and others are also frequently used by artists and companies in the arts. You will also want to decide which platforms—the marketplaces and related applications on top of the protocols, described more below—interest you. You may decide to choose a platform first or to work across multiple platforms and underlying protocols.

Many NFT artworks are minted on the Ethereum protocol. As discussed in Chapter 1, because of the naming convention based on numbered proposals for new token standards on the Ethereum blockchain an NFT is a token that is created and directed by a smart contract, as in the ERC-721 (with "ERC" standing for "Ethereum Request for Comments"). Other blockchains have their own standards (e.g., FA2 for Tezos). While Ethereum has long planned to move to Proof of Stake, it still uses Proof of Work. Many artists have chosen to use other protocols with lower environmental cost. Ethereum also has high transaction costs because one has to pay "gas" fees to mint an NFT. This is the cost of incentivizing miners of cryptocurrency to include your transaction. It is a cost of verifying the transaction—meaning the cost of listing or "minting" your NFT on the blockchain—and securing the network. Gas was originally designed to make it costly and therefore hard for a bad actor to take over the network, but transaction costs have proved very high when the network is busy, leading artists to explore other protocols.[60]

Keys and Wallets

The first step in minting an NFT is to get a wallet. A wallet is a software or hardware device that allows you to store your private keys—or sets of private keys using a "seed" structure. You use the private key to access what you own. If we consider a blockchain as a virtual computer, access to it is gated by private keys instead of user names and passwords. Private keys work in tandem with public keys, which serve as addresses. If you lose your private key, you've generally lost the asset.

The simplest way to establish a wallet is through a web browser plug-in such as MetaMask. MetaMask stores your private keys using your browser, and then you can link the MetaMask wallet (or the wallet of a similar system) to the platform where you are selling or purchasing NFTs. You will need the wallet to pay the gas fees of minting your NFT. Many platforms require you to pay the fees in the cryptocurrency of the blockchain protocol—BTC for the Bitcoin protocol, ETH for the Ethereum protocol, XTZ for Tezos, and so on—while some platforms will allow you to pay with a credit card or purchase cryptocurrency on the platform with a credit card.

Especially if you own a lot of cryptocurrency, but also for anyone, you may get a hardware wallet made by a company such as Ledger to store your private keys. In addition to storing keys, the wallet can send messages to, and receive messages from, blockchains. Hopefully a hardware wallet is "cold" (rather than "hot"), meaning it does not touch the Internet. Instead, it runs transactions offline and then sends them over a USB or Bluetooth connection to a computer that then relays the messages to a blockchain. While there is a property risk of someone accessing the physical wallet and possibly extracting private keys, hardware wallets have to date been considered more secure than software wallets. If you are collecting NFTs that you need to insure, you need to take care with the encryption of the type of wallet you are using. Caroline Taylor, the founder of Appraisal Bureau, has developed proprietary software to evaluate insurance risk and appraisal value of NFTs. The security of one's wallet can be a factor in such an analysis.[61] There are very simple risks, like losing a hardware wallet or, again, losing a private key. Someone with early crypto wealth—known as a "whale"—or anyone else might have their private key in a number of places with the security of a safety deposit box, a flame-resistant piece of metal, and so on. The private key and the wallet are fascinating vulnerabilities, and this is a fast-developing area of software, of secure blockchain protocol, and of platform design.

Importantly, wallets store your private keys, which allow access to the NFTs associated with the works you own. Thus, if we apply the idea of collections management and stewardship of traditional artworks to NFTs, one of the key responsibilities of NFT stewardship is secure storage of the image file itself. One can own an NFT and have it point to a dead URL, meaning the link where the image file was stored no longer works for any reason such as a lapsed website controlled by a third party. Thus, there are a growing number of services to store NFTs. One of the main systems of secure storage is the InterPlanetary File System (IPFS), a storage and data-sharing protocol that is considered both reliable and distributed across a peer-to-peer network of computers embodying the ideals of decentralization and lack of reliance on centralized authorities. Many NFT marketplaces—NFT platforms, as below—actually have their own centralized databases that store the NFTs, so that if the marketplace goes down the NFTs are not accessible. Some marketplaces, such as Foundation and SuperRare, list their NFTs on IPFS, and companies such as Pinata and ClubNFT offer NFT storage. It is one more factor to consider both as an artist and as a collector.

Platforms

The platform is like a storefront or marketplace. Large platforms such as OpenSea are the shopping malls of NFTs, across art and other categories and across primary and secondary markets. When you are considering which platform to use, there are many different factors that include aesthetics. SuperRare, Foundation, and others are curated or require an artist to have an invitation from a member, whereas other platforms, such as Nifty Gateway, have curated "drops" of NFTs but allow anyone to mint.

Two key risks that are important to consider when choosing a platform are wallet or custodial risk and intellectual property risk. For instance, Nifty Gateway uses its own group wallet to issue artworks, which defeats the purpose of having a record of an NFT's digital provenance from the artist's studio; the platform puts many artists' studios in one group.[62] Relatedly, collectors will want to decide their comfort with the custodial wallets some platforms have. To embrace blockchain as a decentralized technology is, strictly speaking, to keep one's own wallet, but for beginners it may be simpler for some to allow the platform to take on a more centralized role.

Secondly, it's important to understand the intellectual property of the platform. While many of us may not read the terms and conditions when we update our mobile phone operating systems, in this case, if you are going to mint or collect seriously, it matters that you understand the intellectual property parameters both of the platform and of the NFT collection you are purchasing. Are you buying a license to an asset or the asset itself? What rights do you have? As discussed in Chapter 3, for some NFT families such as *CryptoPunks*, collectors own commercial rights, whereas for other NFTs, collectors have limited exhibition rights. Owning commercial rights would be highly unusual in the traditional art market, where those rights—copyright, creation of derivative works—are typically retained by the artist. Other factors to consider include the transaction fees that a platform takes—typically 3 to 5 percent—and whether the platform offers a resale royalty to artists when their work is resold.

There are many different platforms to explore, including OpenSea, Rarible, SuperRare, Foundation, Nifty Gateway, Art Blocks, Hic et Nunc (on Tezos), and many others. Some traditional contemporary art galleries have developed platform partnerships, such as Pace Gallery's partnership with Art Blocks. And Monegraph, the company founded by Kevin McCoy and Anil Dash, now works with galleries to let them set up their own parameters around resale royalties and other features within the Monegraph system.

There are also registries—such as Artory or Fairchain—that may operate marketplaces but take a provenance-first approach to listing artworks in ways that are enabled by, but not led by, NFTs and blockchain. In addition, in the web3 space of developing an artist-led collaborative economy, companies such as Metaversal produce artists' projects, and Rally.io allows artists to develop their own tokens.

Smart Contracts and DAOs

If you have minted an NFT, it is governed by the smart contracts associated with it. For example, if a platform pays you a resale royalty, a smart contract can automate that—for instance, if this work sells, automatically give 10 percent of the selling price back to the originating wallet. Smart contracts can be designed to do anything, and they can also be put together into decentralized autonomous organizations (DAOs) that operate as automated organizations. Groups of artists have used DAOs to pool resources and then invest larger sums in one another's work, and groups of collectors have used DAOs to purchase work as a collective. DAOs highlight the larger theme of governance, that is, of designing the mechanisms by which decisions are made across a collective.

In summary, you can get started easily with a MetaMask wallet, a bit of cryptocurrency for minting costs, and a choice of platform. Take care with storing private keys—or deciding, at least in the short term, to trust them to a platform as caretaker, recognizing the trust placed in a central administrator.

NOTES

1   Deborah Kass, Amalia Mesa-Bains, Meleko Mokgosi, Wendy Red Star, and Carrie Mae Weems (moderator), "What Does Diversifying Collections Mean to Artists" (panel, Deaccessioning after 2020 Symposium, Syracuse University, March 18, 2021, https://www.youtube.com/watch?v=mlizofXMYq4). For more on the symposium, see https://vpa.syr.edu/wp-content/uploads/Session-Recording-Links-1.pdf.

2   Ben Davis, "I Looked Through All 5,000 Images in Beeple's $69 Million Magnum Opus. What I Found Isn't So Pretty," *Artnet News,* March 17, 2021, https://news.artnet.com/opinion/beeple-everydays-review-1951656, accessed June 28, 2022.

3   Author interview with Joseph Bonneau, September 21, 2021. Any unattributed quotations are from the MCA Denver program series.

4   Wolma Woo, "'Leonardo da Vinci' Puts Mona Lisa Painting on the Blockchain," *Bitcoinist,* June 11, 2018, https://bitcoinist.com/leonardo-da-vinci-mona-lisa-blockchain-verisart/. For the listing on the Verisart blockchain, see https://verisart.com/works/23f2c64a-08c6-4a42-8013-84ac8422dffb.

5   For more information on *Citizens United v. Federal Election Commission*, see Tim Lau, "Citizens United Explained," Brennan Center, December 12, 2019, https://www.brennancenter.org/our-work/research-reports/citizens-united-explained.

6   Author interview with Kevin McCoy, September 14, 2021.

7   Sol LeWitt, "Paragraphs on Conceptual Art," *Artforum*, Summer 1967, https://www.artforum.com/print/196706/paragraphs-on-conceptual-art-36719.

8   Author interviews with Chris Vacchio, September 13 and October 25, 2021.

9   Kabir Jhala, "WTAF? Beeple NFT Work Sells for Astonishing $69.3M at Christie's after Flurry of Last-Minute Bids Nearly Crashes Website," *The Art Newspaper,* March 11, 2021, https://www.theartnewspaper.com/2021/03/11/wtaf-beeple-nft-work-sells-for-astonishing-dollar693m-at-christies-after-flurry-of-last-minute-bids-nearly-crashes-website.

10   Stuart Haber and Scott Stornetta, "How to Time-Stamp a Digital Document," *Journal of Cryptology* 3 (January 1991): 99–111.

11   Cambridge Center for Alternative Finance, "Cambridge Bitcoin Electricity Consumption Index," https://ccaf.io/cbeci/index/comparisons.

12   Finn Brunton, *Digital Cash: The Unknown History of the Anarchists, Utopians, and Technologists Who Created Cryptocurrency* (Princeton, NJ: Princeton University Press, 2019), 66-79.

13   Hans Ulrich Obrist and Vitalik Buterin, "Hello, Vitalik Buterin," *Tank Magazine* 74 (Spring 2018): https://tankmagazine.com/issue-74/features/vitalik-buterin. See also D. T. Max, "The Art of Conversation," *The New Yorker,* December 8, 2014, 64–73.

14   Underlying interview footage of Hans Ulrich Obrist interviewing Vitalik Buterin used, with grateful permission, in the MCA Denver Presents: Putting the Fun in Non-Fungible Tokens Series event "Episode 1: Origin Stories," October 13, 2021, https://www.youtube.com/watch?v=uDX5nYCFG2k.

15   Michael Govan, Fred Sandback, Marianne Stockebrand, and Gianfranco Verna, "2002 Conversation," Fred Sandback Archive, 2002, https://www.fredsandbackarchive.org/texts-2002-conversation. The live conversation was a program at the Chinati Foundation, Marfa, Texas, on October 6, 2001. It was also published in *Chinati Foundation Newsletter*, October 2002, 26–32.

16   Lauren van Haaften-Schick and Amy Whitaker, "From the Artist's Contract to the Blockchain Ledger: New Forms of Artists' Funding Using Equity and Resale Royalties," *Journal of Cultural Economics* 46, no. 2 (June 2022): 287–315.

17   Lauren van Haaften-Schick, Oxford Handbooks Online, "Conceptualizing Artists' Rights: Circulation of the Siegelaub-Projansky Agreement Through Art and Law," https://www.oxfordhandbooks.com/view/10.1093/oxfordhb/9780199935352.001.0001/oxfordhb-9780199935352-e-27.

18   Nicole Wilson, *National Debt Project*, http://www.nationaldebtproject.com.

19   Chris Vacchio, author interview, September 13, 2021.

20   Kevin McCoy, author interview, September 14, 2021.

21   Luis Jacob, *Commerce by Artists* (Toronto: Art Metropole, 2011), 16–21.

22   Holland Cotter, "700-Hour Silent Opera Finale at MoMA," *The New York Times*, May 30, 2010.

23   Lewis Hyde, *The Gift* (New York: Random House, 1983).

24   Author interview with Kevin and Jennifer McCoy, September 14, 2021.

25   Kevin and Jennifer McCoy, *Public Key/Private Key*, [film and art project], New York: Whitney Museum of American Art, 2019, https://whitney.org/exhibitions/public-key-private-key.

26   Wallace Ludel, "Kevin McCoy and Sotheby's Sued Over Sale of Early NFT, *The Art Newspaper*, February 4, 2022, https://www.theartnewspaper.com/2022/02/04/sothebys-kevin-mccoy-lawsuit-quantum-nft.

27   Kevin McCoy author interview, September 14, 2021.

28   1989: Infoplease, "U.S. Households with Computers and Internet Use," https://www.infoplease.com/math-science/computers-internet/us-households-with-computers-and-internet-use-1984-2014.
2019: Clare McAndrew, *Art Basel Market Report 2022* (Zurich: Art Basel and UBS, 2022), 14.
2021: McAndrew, *Art Basel Market Report 2022*, 14.

29   König Galerie, "*The Artist Is Online*," https://koenig.art/collections/nfts.

30   Nicole Wilson, "Ötzi Terms and Conditions," Praise Shadows Art Gallery, https://praiseshadows.com/otziterms-conditions/.

31   Larva Labs, "CryptoPunks," https://www.larvalabs.com/cryptopunks.

32   In March 2021, the Dutch government gave the museum a 2.5 million euro grant, covering the lion's share of the 2.85 million euros lost in the scam. "Museum Gets Subsidy to Buy Constable after Losing €2.85m in Scam," DutchNews.nl, March 23, 2021, https://www.dutchnews.nl/news/2021/03/museum-gets-subsidy-to-buy-constable-after-losing-e2-85m-in-scam/.

33   Yuga Labs, "Yuga Labs Acquires CryptoPunks and Meebits and Gives Commercial Rights to the Community," Mirror.xyz, March 11, 2022, https://mirror.xyz/0xEc9f53fA69682833FBd760C104B5D61aE29221E0/Km81y6Mc3O5LzS0wnrghVIV0HnZgLOd4wsnfcGw3_2I.

34   McAndrew, *Art Basel Market Report 2022*. See also Clare McAndrew, *Art Basel Market Report 2021* (Zurich: Art Basel and UBS, 2021), https://artbasel.com/about/initiatives/the-art-market.

35   Muriel Quancard and Amy Whitaker, "Digital Provenance and the Wallet Problem," *Outland*, June 17, 2022, https://outland.art/digital-provenance-and-the-wallet-problem/.

36   The formal title of the sale was *This Changed Everything: Source Code for the WWW x Tim Berners-Lee, an NFT.* https://www.sothebys.com/en/buy/auction/2021/this-changed-everything-source-code-for-www-x-tim-berners-lee-an-nft/source-code-for-the-www.

37   Harrison C. White and Cynthia A. White, *Canvases and Careers: Institutional Change in the French Painting World* (Chicago: University of Chicago Press, 1993). Jennifer C. Lena, *Entitled: Discriminating Tastes and the Expansion of the Arts* (Princeton, NJ: Princeton University Press, 2021).

38   Bruce Sterling, "Social Codes at Feral File," *Medium*, April 8, 2021, https://bruces.medium.com/social-codes-at-feralfile-399840a43757.

39   Author correspondence with Judy Mam, June 29, 2022.

40   For the white paper introducing the "Invisible Economy," see: Beatriz Ramos and Yehudit Mam, "Introducing the Invisible Economy," *Medium,* May 17, 2020, https://powerdada.medium.com/the-invisible-economy-db46897d4f07.

41   Massimo Franceschet and Sparrow Read, "The Inconvenient Truth About Secondary Markets, Part II," *Medium*, December 14, 2020, https://powerdada.medium.com/the-inconvenient-truth-about-secondary-markets-part-ii-6c148a917a08.

42   Amy Whitaker, *Art Thinking* (New York: Harper Business, 2016).

43 Pablo Helguera, Michael Mandiberg, William Powhida, Amy Whitaker, and Caroline Woolard, *The Social Life of Artistic Property* (Hudson, NY: Publication Studio, 2014).

44 Amy Whitaker and Roman Kräussl, "Fractional Equity, Blockchain, and the Future of Creative Work," *Management Science* 66, no. 10: 4,594–611.

45 Nati Linares and Caroline Woolard, *Solidarity Not Charity: Grantmaking in the Solidarity Economy* (New York: Grantmakers in the Arts, 2021), https://art.coop/report/.

46 Felwine Sarr and Bénédicte Savoy, *The Restitution of African Cultural Heritage: Toward a New Relational Ethics*, https://www.about-africa. de/images/sonstiges/2018/sarr_savoy_en.pdf.

47 Amy Whitaker, Anne Bracegirdle, Susan de Menil, Michelle Ann Gitlitz, and Lena Saltos, "Art, Antiquities, and Blockchain: New Approaches to the Restitution of Cultural Heritage," *International Journal of Cultural Policy* 27, no. 3 (2020): 312–29. The Art and Antiquities Blockchain Consortium website is https://aabconsortium.org.

48 Van Haaften-Schick, "Conceptualizing Artists' Rights." See also Seth Siegelaub and Robert Projansky, "The Artist's Reserved Rights Transfer and Sale Agreement," https:// primaryinformation.org/product/siegelaub-the-artists-reserved-rights-transfer-and-sale-agreement/.

49 Robin Pogrebin, "Tech Start-Up Aims to Get Artists Royalties for Resale, *The New York Times*, March 23, 2022. Robert Rauschenberg Foundation, "Rauschenberg Medical Emergency Grants," https://www.rauschenbergfoundation. org/programs/grants/rauschenberg-emergency-grants.

50 TRANSFER, "*Pieces of Me*," http:// transfergallery.com/pieces-of-me/.

51 Robin Pogrebin and Siddhartha Mitter, "They Pooled Their Art to Create a Nest Egg. They Say It Was a Mistake," *The New York Times*, July 27, 2021, https://www.nytimes.com/2021/07/27/ arts/design/artist-pension-trust.html.

52 For more information on the history of the Artist's Contract, including its growth out of the Art Workers' Coalition, see van Haaften-Schick, "Conceptualizing Artists' Rights."

53 Strategic National Arts Alumni Project, *Aggregate Frequency Report*, http://snaap.indiana.edu/ pdf/2017/SNAAP15_16_17_Aggregate_Report. pdf; Roger Schonfeld and Mariët Westermann with Liam Sweeney, *The Andrew W. Mellon Foundation Art Museum Staff Demographic Survey*, July 28, 2015, https://mellon.org/media/ filer_public/ba/99/ba99e53a-48d5-4038-80e1-66f9ba1c020e/awmf_museum_diversity_report_aamd_7-28-15.pdf.

54 *Art Museum Staff Demographic Survey*, July 28, 2015, https://mellon.org/media/ filer_public/ba/99/ba99e53a-48d5-4038-80e1-66f9ba1c020e/awmf_museum_diversity_report_aamd_7-28-15.pdf

55 Christopher Turner, "At the Fondazione Prada, Painting Refuses to Play Dead," *Apollo*, July 27, 2021, https://www.apollo-magazine.com/peter-fischli-painting-fondazione-prada/.

56 Reena Devi, "Marina Abramović on the Eve of Her First NFT: Web3 Is 'Undoubtedly the Future,'" *ARTnews*, June 13, 2022, https://www.artnews.com/art-news/news/ marina-abramovic-nft-the-hero-basel-interview1234631675-1234631675/.

57 Pace Verso, "Jeff Koons Unveils 'Moon Phases' NFT Project," March 29, 2022, https://www. pacegallery.com/journal/jeff-koons-unveils-moon-phases-nft-project/.

58 MCA Denver, *Clarissa Tossin: Falling from Earth*," https://mcadenver.org/exhibitions/ clarissa-tossin.

59 Betsy Huete, "In Houston, Artist Clarissa Tossin Ponders the Colonial Implications of the 21st-Century Space Race," *ARTnews*, March 18, 2022, https://www.artnews.com/art-news/ artists/clarissa-tossin-moody-center-houston-exhibition-interview-1234622226/.

60 Vitalik Buterin, "Ethereum Whitepaper: A Next-Generation Smart Contract and Decentralized Application Platform," *Ethereum.org*, 2014, https://ethereum.org/ en/whitepaper/.

61 Kevin T. Dugan, "How Museums Are Trying to Figure Out What NFT Art Is Worth," *New York*, January 23, 2022, https://nymag.com/ intelligencer/2022/01/how-museums-are-trying-to-figure-out-what-nft-art-is-worth.html.

62 Quancard and Whitaker, "Digital Provenance and the Wallet Problem," *Outland Art,* June 17, 2022, https://outland.art/digital-provenance-and-the-wallet-problem/.

126

ACKNOWLEDGMENTS

WE WISH TO RECOGNIZE the many individuals who contributed thoughtfully and materially to the development of this publication and without whom this book would not have been possible.

The project began with a seemingly innocuous comment from Zach Morin encouraging MCA Denver to produce a program exploring the topic of NFTs. We are grateful to Zach for seeding the idea, and to Veronica Roberts, director of the Cantor Arts Center, for bringing the two of us together as collaborators and then co-authors to launch this.

Beginning with those who participated in the production of the original "NFTs-WTF?" and "Putting the Fun in Non-Fungible Tokens" series at MCA Denver, we warmly thank the production team of Courtney Law, Cheyenne Michaels, and Kelly O'Connell. As well, we wish to acknowledge everyone who contributed to the framing and relaying of the many stories of NFTs: Heather Bhandari, Marja Bloem, Joseph Bonneau, Anne Bracegirdle, Eduardo Burillo, Valentina Castellani, Dmitri Cherniak, Lenka Clayton, Nanne Dekking, Susan de Menil, Saskia Draxler, Cheryl Finley, Adriana Fowler, Andrea Fraser, Masoud Golsorkhi, Art Grayson, Stuart Haber, Matt Hall, Cassandra Hatton, Tehching Hsieh, Max Kendrick, Roman Kräussl, Sandy Lee, Sofia LeWitt, John Maeda, Judy Mam, Jennifer McCoy, Kevin McCoy, Sean Moss-Pultz, Michael Nguyễn, Kelani Nichole, Heather Nolin, Hans Ulrich Obrist, Jenny Polak, Beatriz Ramos, Pablo Rodriguez-Fraile, Claire Schlaikjer, Dread Scott, Eddie Sikazwe, Lesley Silverman, Nicolas Smirnoff, Marcia Stornetta, Scott Stornetta, Anton Stuebner, Elise Swopes, Caroline Taylor, Chris Torres, Chris Vacchio, Lauren van Haaften-Schick, Addie Wagenknecht, Tricia Wang, John Watkinson, Nicole Wilson, and David Yermack.

One of the key distinguishing aspects of our "Putting the Fun in Non-Fungible Tokens" series was the use of introductory videos that brought the central themes of each episode to the surface. We wish to thank Adam Lipsius, Mike Bloom, Joseph Bramer, Patrick Dingman, Tina Pacheco, Gabriel Royand, Ashley Vaughn, and Lily Weisberg for the care with which they produced and edited these.

We also wish to thank Sotheby's, and especially Nina del Rio and Molly Nelson, for their crucial support of this project.

For this publication, we are immensely grateful to the publisher, Charles Miers, for believing in the possibility of this book and to Isabel Venero for her indefatigable efforts to help get it across the finish line. Thanks, as well, are due to our graphic designer, Sarah Gifford, for her elegant design. It has been an honor to work with this multi-talented team.

April Zhu provided invaluable research assistance with this book and masterful organization of the production and copyright clearance process. We wish to recognize her thorough and foundational contributions.

We are grateful to Judd Grossman, Stuart Haber, and Sean Moss-Pultz for lending especially kind expertise to this project, and to the many artists, gallerists, researchers, and others who allowed us to tell their stories and who generously shared their work and graciously supported the production of the book, including those who wished to remain anonymous.

Amy also is grateful for her original introduction to blockchain in 2014 via the company Bitmark (which hosts Feral File), where she continues to serve as an advisor. She is also an investor in Fairchain, whose nonprofit Fund for Working Artists is mentioned in this book.

Nora wishes to express her gratitude to the entire staff and board of MCA Denver for lending such meaningful support to this project.

Lastly, we wish to recognize the generosity and curiosity that defined our collaboration and gratefully thank each other for journeying through this project with warmth and humor.

PHOTO CREDITS

Cover and page 54: Courtesy of the artist. Back cover and page 77: Courtesy of the collectors. Pages 2 and 88–89: Courtesy of the artists. Page 6: Courtesy of the artist. Pages 10–11: © 2021 Christie's Images Limited. Page 13: Courtesy of the artist. Pages 24 and 26–27: © Estate of Sol LeWitt, 2022. Photo by Kevin Kennefick, courtesy of Mass MoCA and the LeWitt Collection. (First drawn by: P. Giacchi, A. Giamasco, G. Mosca. First installation: Sperone Gallery, Turin, Italy and Museo di Torino, Turin, Italy). Pages 28 and 29: © Estate of Sol LeWitt, 2022. Courtesy of the LeWitt Collection. Page 30: Reproduced under fair use owing to impossibility of contacting Satoshi Nakamoto. Image courtesy of Sean Moss-Pultz. Page 32: Nyan Cat Image is a © and registered trademark of Christopher Orlando Torres, used under license. Courtesy of the artist. Page 36: Courtesy of Drs. Stuart Haber and Scott Stornetta. Page 37: © 1990 Advance Local Media. All rights reserved. Used under license. Page 41: Courtesy of *Tank Magazine*, Vitalik Buterin, and Hans Ulrich Obrist. Page 43: Estate of Fred Sandback; Courtesy David Zwirner Gallery, New York. Page 47: Courtesy of the artist. Photo: TJ Proechel. Pages 54 and 55: © Tehching Hsieh. Courtesy of the artist. Page 56: Courtesy of the artist and Catharine Clark Gallery. Pages 62–63: Courtesy of the artist and KÖNIG GALERIE. Page 64: Courtesy of the artist. Page 65: Courtesy of the artist. Photo: Kelly & Massa Photography. Page 68: Courtesy of the artist and Cristin Tierney Gallery. Page 70: Courtesy of the artist. Photo: TJ Proechel. Pages 74 and 91: Courtesy of the artist and Feral File. Page 101: Courtesy Whitaker, Kräussl, and *Management Science*. Pages 106 and 107: Courtesy Stichting Egress Foundation, Amsterdam, Estate of Seth Siegelaub, and Marja Bloem. Pages 114–15: Courtesy of the artist. Photo: Nash Baker.

First published in the United States of America in 2023 by
Rizzoli Electa, A Division of
Rizzoli International Publications, Inc.
300 Park Avenue South
New York, NY 10010
www.rizzoliusa.com

in association with

MCA Denver
1485 Delgany Street
Denver, CO 80202
mcadenver.org

Copyright © 2023 Amy Whitaker and Nora Burnett Abrams

Publisher: Charles Miers
Editor: Isabel Venero
Production Manager: Kaija Markoe
Designer: Sarah Gifford

Printed in China

2023 2024 2025 2026 / 10 9 8 7 6 5 4 3 2 1
ISBN: 978-0-8478-9936-4
Library of Congress Control Number on file

Visit us online:
Facebook.com/RizzoliNewYork
Twitter: @Rizzoli_Books
Instagram.com/RizzoliBooks
Pinterest.com/RizzoliBooks
Youtube.com/user/RizzoliNY

Front cover
Addie Wagenknecht, *Rainbow Eugene Man* (detail), 2021. Digital work utilizing sext and "dick pics" received in Instagram DMs from 2015 to 2018 in a body of paintings using custom computational brushes.

Back cover
Matt Hall and John Watkinson (Larva Labs), collection of *CryptoPunks*, 2017. Algorithmically generated collectible characters and associated non-fungible token. From left to right: Top row: *CryptoPunk* 8066, 8360, 7649. Second row: 4019, 4346, 4298. Third row: 7219, 5361, 6255. Bottom row: 1348, 0382

Page 2
Matt Hall and John Watkinson (Larva Labs), *Autoglyphs* (detail, no. 1), 2019, on-chain algorithms that serve conceptually as "instructions" that generate drawings.